U2

Until the End of the World

G:

Published in 2025
by Gemini Gift Books
Part of Gemini Books Group

Based in Woodbridge and London

Marine House, Tide Mill Way,
Woodbridge, Suffolk IP12 1AP
United Kingdom

www.geminibooks.com

Text © 2025 Bradley Morgan
Design and layout © 2025 Gemini Gift Books Ltd

Bradley Morgan has asserted his moral rights to be
identified as the author and illustrator of this Work
in accordance with the Copyright, Designs and
Patents Act of 1988.

ISBN 978-1-78675-165-2

A CIP catalogue record for this book is available
from the British Library.

Manufacturer's EU Representative:
Eurolink Compliance Limited, 25 Herbert Place,
Dublin, D02 AY86, Republic of Ireland.
admin@eurolink-europe.ie

Printed in China

10 9 8 7 6 5 4 3 2 1

U2

Until the End of the World

BRADLEY MORGAN

Contents

> ## "We're a band from the north side of Dublin called the U2"

Bono told a roaring home-town crowd while on tour in 2018 as they welcomed him and his bandmates, the Edge, Adam Clayton and Larry Mullen Jr, back to the bubblin' city by the sea. As the launch pad to blast off into 'I Will Follow', their first single released nearly four decades earlier, it is a refrain he has returned to many times before to connect with fans, Bono's reference to the band as the U2 a callback to when the project first began. No matter how far and high they may go, they always find themselves with their feet on the ground, right back where it all began. More than just an introduction for the band, it is a bold declaration of who they are, where they come from and where they are going.

U2's origin is a humble one, with the friends rehearsing for the first time in a kitchen after responding to the flyer Larry posted on their school's bulletin board. It was 1976, a tumultuous period in Ireland for everyone, let alone those seeking a career in music. With the sectarian violence being waged in Northern Ireland at times finding its way into their backyard, and with limited opportunities for musicians to take their sound beyond the pubs, U2's boyhood years as a band represented defiance, crafting a unique appeal amidst a cultural and social landscape that offered little and promised nothing.

The horizon looked a shade brighter when the band, performing as The Hype after changing it from their original name, Feedback, won first place in a talent contest in Limerick in 1978. The grand prize was £500 and a demo recording contract. Though the results of that demo session would be rough due to their inexperience and limited abilities, it instilled a new-found confidence within the group. Or – at the very least – enough motivation to keep trying.

Their friend Steve Averill, singer in The Radiators from Space (a pioneering group in Ireland's fledgling punk scene), suggested the name U2 because of its ambiguity and open-endedness. The band would go on to make a name for themselves in the local music scene performing in small clubs and growing their reputation with audiences as a dynamic and engaging live act. Their commitment to the craft would serve them well on their path to becoming one of the biggest bands in the world. With the arrival of punk in Ireland during the late 1970s, the

L-R: The Edge, Adam Clayton, Larry Mullen Jnr, Bono. U2 in Belgium, 1980.

members of U2 could finally envision a do-it-yourself space in which to forge an identity; if four kids from Dublin could do it, so could you.

The early 1980s would see U2's emergence from the conflict they felt within their personal and cultural identities, as they sought to bring their Irish iteration of bombastic punk stylings to new audiences. Their debut album *Boy* explores the complexities of boyhood innocence amidst tragedy and isolation. U2 would continue this theme for *October*, attempting to find the balance between their art and faith. With the success of *War*, they would earn renown as a band with something much bigger and more profound to say.

By the end of the decade, U2 would become, as *Time* put it, rock's hottest ticket. *The Unforgettable Fire* saw the band embrace the avant-garde in the first of several artistic shifts, thanks to a blossoming relationship with Brian Eno and Daniel Lanois. After U2 were propelled to the world stage with their breakthrough at Live Aid, they embarked on a musical journey that helped them better understand their own spirit. *The Joshua Tree* allowed U2 to go deep into the heartland of America, an experience that revealed to them their own Irishness, after witnessing the conflict between the country's reality and the myths it upholds. By the release of *Rattle and Hum*, realizing they were about to lose their way back home, U2 needed new dreams.

As the Iron Curtain fell, and a new Europe burst forth, U2 sought to reinvent themselves in the 1990s by stepping into the Technicolor flourish of electronic dance music. Though, they too would almost collapse. Nearly on the verge of breaking up over creative differences, until one song became their saving grace, *Achtung Baby* revealed U2 could redefine their own music while still being innovative. U2 would continue experimenting with their sound throughout the decade, with them pushing their musical boundaries for *Zooropa* while deconstructing their band's dynamic for the Warholesque commentary of *Pop*.

With the dawn of a new millennium came the opportunity for U2 to rebuild themselves once again, returning to their traditional sound and rediscovering the joy of four friends playing music together in a room. Coming to terms with their emotional and

Daniel Lanois, who won the 1987 Producer Of The Year award, was at the controls for U2's *The Joshua Tree*. Following spread: U2 perform perform at the Mediolanum Forum in Milan, Italy, 2018.

personal baggage, *All That You Can't Leave Behind* allowed U2 to strip away the excess and focus on the simplicity of what matters most in life. Further exploring their musical philosophy, U2 drew from their post-punk roots for *How to Dismantle an Atomic Bomb* and reached towards the unknown, drawing influences from world music for *No Line on the Horizon*. It was a decade that would represent a journey in search of soul.

As they were entering their fourth decade together by the mid-2010s, U2 felt the way to move forward was by going back to before there even was a band. *Songs of Innocence* took its inspiration from the violence and emotional turmoil of 1970s Dublin, reflecting on all the first experiences that set them on their path. Its companion, *Songs of Experience*, showed their appreciation for all those who joined them along the way. On *Songs of Surrender*, U2 would showcase the strength of their songs and their legacy, capturing an intimacy within their earlier work to better understand their relationship with their former and current selves.

Life can be an incredible journey if you know what is important in it. For U2, it was an innocence that kept them motivated to break out of a dull and listless existence fraught with cynicism and fear. It became the key to their success and the guiding star in their journey as artists and as people. As with any journey, it is never about the destination but rather the steps we take and the path that we follow.

Fifty years. Four friends. One journey. This is the story of U2.

At a photoshoot in Ireland, 1981. Following spread: Bono performing with U2 at the Maysfield Leisure Centre in Belfast, N. Ireland, 1982.

1

Another Time, Another Place

"Drummer seeks musicians to form band."

When a 14-year-old student posted this note on the community board of his school, he had no expectations of what would come from it. The idea for him was just to get some friends together and have fun playing music. There were only a few years left until school would be over, and then the seemingly limitless opportunity and freedom of childhood would soon be swallowed up by the monster that lay in wait on the other side of graduation: getting a job. Larry Mullen Jr's musical journey had begun when he pinned that notice.

'This odd group of people convened in my kitchen in Artane. And that's where it started.'

On 25 September 1976, a group of teenagers who had answered Larry's notice squeezed into the kitchen of his home, barely fitting in all their equipment. Driven with naive excitement at just how big a noise they could make, the audition in Larry's kitchen was a chance for some kids to show their love for groups like The Rolling Stones and T. Rex by banging out messy versions of their favourite songs. 'We didn't really have a clue what we were doing,' said Ivan McCormick, who auditioned that day but was too young to make the cut.

This coming together of raw aspirations to make even rawer sounds was an ethos rooted in punk music way before the band would even have any language to describe it as such. While the songs they rehearsed were not typically punk as we think of it, this gathering of misfits used the music they knew and had access to in order to transcend their life growing up in the listless suburbs of mid-1970s Dublin. Though they wouldn't know it, the core of one of rock's most commercially and critically successful groups were playing together for the first time. Such humble beginnings for the band that would become U2 way before they even knew they were U2 to begin with. As Bono said in an early interview, U2 were 'a band before we could play'.

Before they became U2, they were four kids in Dublin dreaming of something more. Larry Mullen Jr, born in Dublin in 1961, started his musical education early in life, learning piano and then drumming before turning ten years old. Larry would go on to perform in several

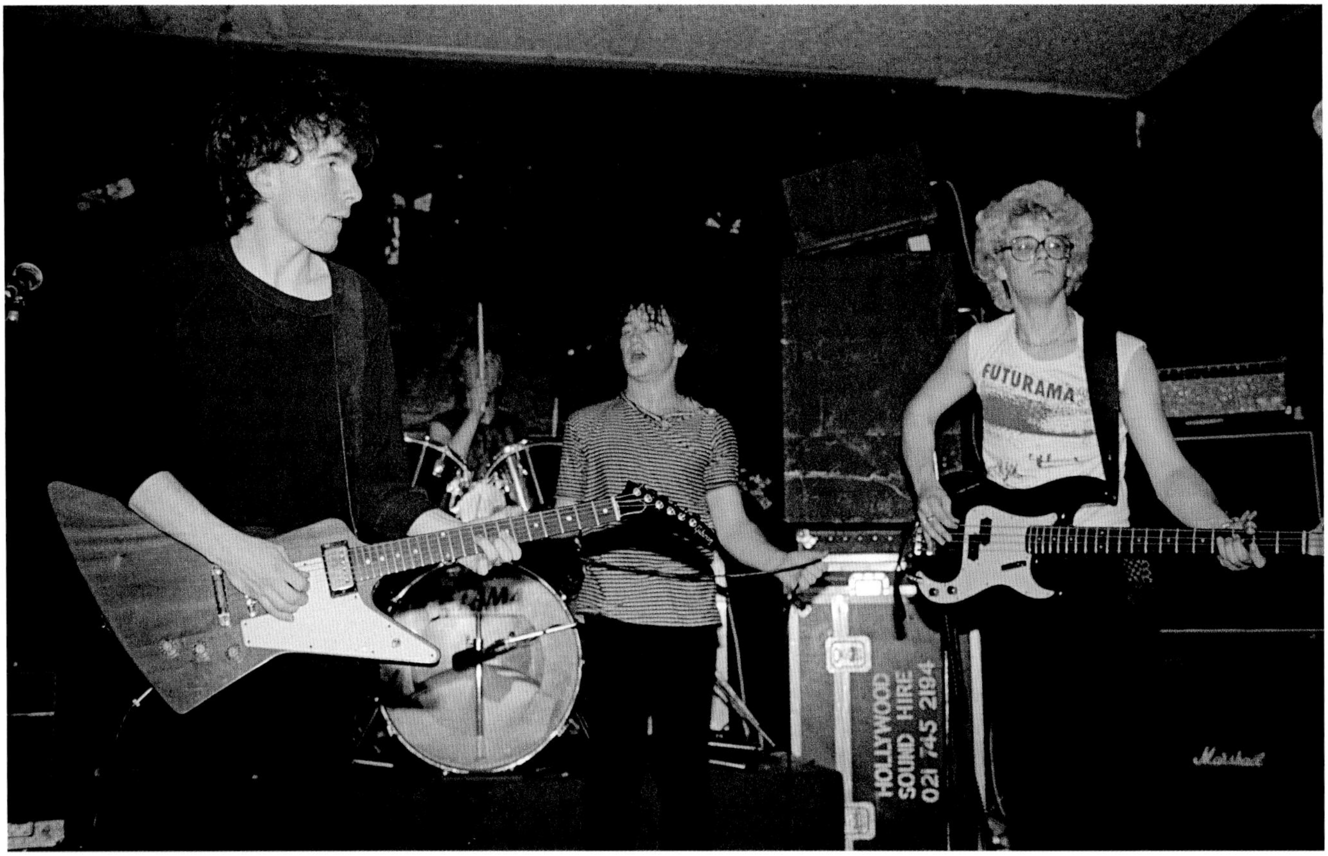
FUTURAMA
HOLLYWOOD
SOUND HIRE
021 745 2194

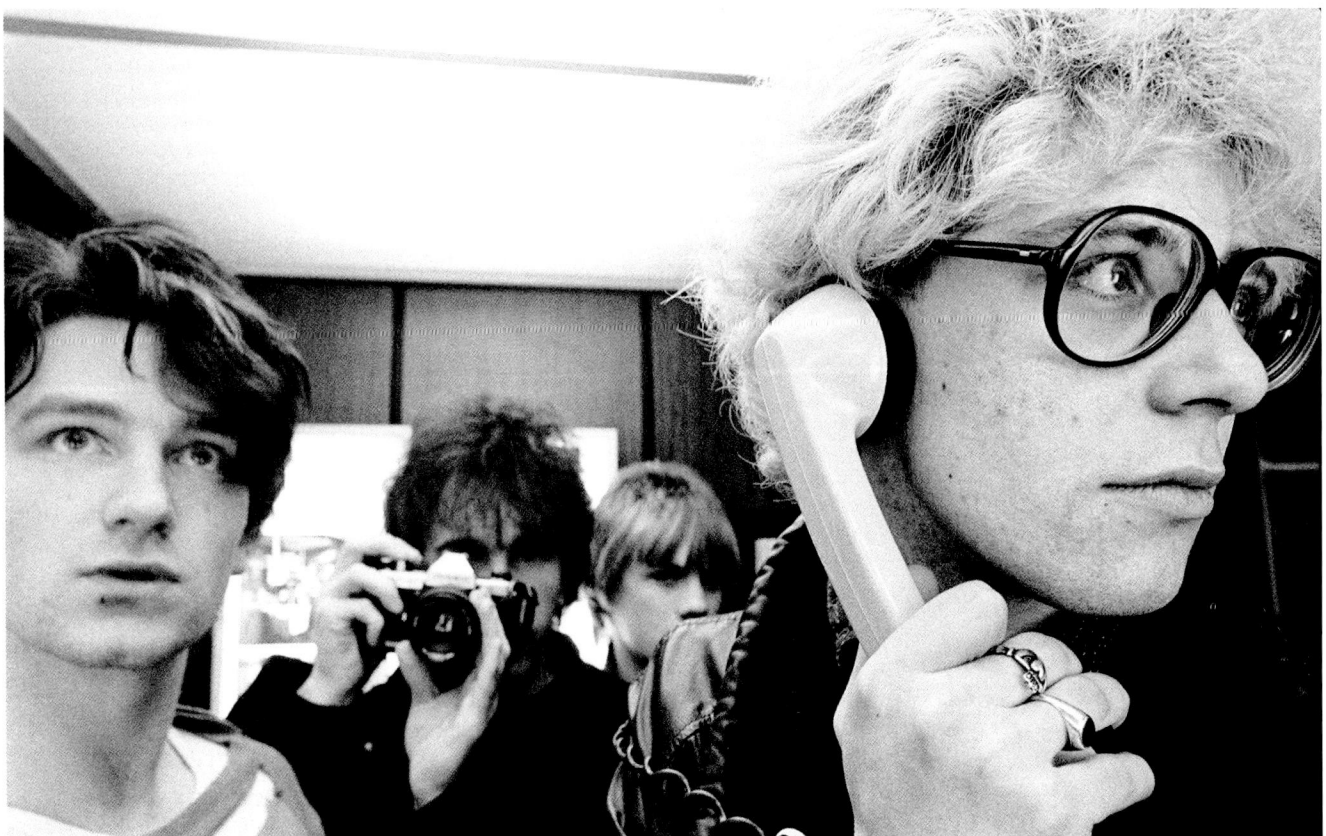

marching bands, first for an all-boys outfit (before quitting over disagreements about his hair length), then performing orchestral percussion in a post office ensemble. Feeling unstimulated by the marching bands and his jazz drumming lessons, Larry sought to discover more interesting musical horizons, which led him to post that note in search of rock 'n' roll.

Larry was a student at Mount Temple Comprehensive School, an interdenominational school unique in its time, as education was generally segregated between Catholics and Protestants. It would be there he would meet the boys that would become his bandmates.

David Evans, later known as the Edge, was born in Essex in the United Kingdom in 1961 before moving to Ireland with his Welsh parents and older brother when he was two years old. David experienced difficulty connecting with his peers due to coming from a different country, particularly one entangled in a complicated history with his new home. This resulted in him having to speak in both Welsh and Irish accents so he could feel understood.

David grew up in the affluent suburb of Malahide, where he became interested in guitar at an early age. After he outgrew his first guitar, a child-sized Spanish model his mother gave him, he purchased his first acoustic from a rummage sale for a pound. When one of his teachers informed him that another student was forming a band, he decided to check it out.

Adam Clayton had also moved to Ireland from England as a child, having been born in Oxfordshire in 1960. Settling in Malahide, both Adam's and David's families were acquainted, well before the two became friends. Unlike Larry and David, Adam's early exposure to music was restricted. Attending a private boarding school in Dalkey, Adam was dismayed to find that pop music was banned, leaving classical music and rock operas like *Jesus Christ Superstar* and *Hair* as his only musical outlets. It was a culture Adam found difficult to understand, making it a challenge to connect with his classmates. It wasn't until he transferred to another private school a few years later that Adam began to make friends through a shared interest in rock music. Though he struggled with school academically and socially, being around other

Opposite top: Live on the Boy Tour in Appeldorn, Germany, 1980.
Opposite bottom: L-R: Bono, The Edge (holding the camera), Larry Mullen Jnr, Adam Clayton, Belgium, 1980.
Above: Larry Mullen Jnr, Belgium, 1980.

Above: Larry Mullen Jnr, The Edge, Bono, band manager Paul McGuinness, Island Records founder Chris Blackwell and Adam Clayton, 1980.
Opposite: Belgium, 1980.

students who liked the same music gave Adam the confidence to buy a cheap acoustic guitar. Adam was later expelled and transferred to Mount Temple where he would meet people who truly shared his musical interests.

Paul Hewson, born in Dublin in 1960 before the world would come to know him as Bono, had music on his mind at a very young age. However, it took time to be realized as his childhood was defined by tragedy. Iris, Paul's mother, suffered a cerebral aneurysm while attending her own father's funeral, collapsing just as his casket was being lowered. Bono, in his memoir *Surrender*, recalled seeing his father carry his mother away through a crowd that 'splits open like a white snooker ball hitting a triangle of colour'. Only 14 years old, it was an event that would have an impact on the rest of his life, greatly affecting his personal and artistic development. After his mother's passing, Paul's home became volatile with melancholic rage. His father and brother never spoke of Iris, and the three men processed their grief by fighting with one another.

The trauma of his early years motivated Paul to discover a different life from the one he had been given. Paul roamed the streets of Dublin as part of a collective called Lypton Village, a surrealist street performance gang started with his friends Derek Rowen and Fionán Hanvey, both of whom later founded the Virgin Prunes under the pseudonyms Guggi and Gavin Friday respectively. Nicknames were a big part of Lypton Village, and Guggi performed the christenings. David was also a member, which is how he came to be known as the Edge possibly because of the angular shape of his head. Paul would go by several aliases in Lypton Village such as Steinhegvanhuysenolegbangbangbang, Huyseman and Bono Vox of O'Connell Street before the latter was eventually shortened to Bono Vox. This came from the name of a local hearing aid shop based on a mistranslation of the Latin phrase for 'good voice', and Paul kept Bono as his official moniker.

Calling themselves Feedback, because they were self-taught and it was the only musical term they knew, the students were eager to make themselves heard. The next thing was to find people who were willing to listen.

Making their public debut at a school talent show, Feedback performed a short set of covers, including Peter Frampton's 'Show Me the Way' and 'Bye Bye Baby' by the Bay City Rollers. Their inexperience and limited repertoire became apparent when, after the crowd chanted for an encore, Feedback returned to play a second rendition of 'Bye Bye Baby'. However, despite their nervousness performing in front of a crowd for the first time, the reception they received from their schoolmates was a revelation to the anxious adolescents. 'It was really a feeling of liberation,' said Bono. 'It's like you've jumped into the sea and discovered you can swim.'

'After that, I think we were a band,' said Larry.

Their first concert at Mount Temple made them aware that they needed to rehearse a lot more to overcome their musical limitations. Thanks to their teachers, they were able to use one of the music rooms at school on Saturdays to practise. When they outgrew that rehearsal space, they relocated to a small cottage in the same graveyard where Bono's mother was buried. In this space they called the 'Yellow House', Feedback began to work on their musical identity. With the pain of his mother's death still lingering and her presence surrounding these rehearsals, Bono felt a kind of clarity. 'Everything changed for me,' he said in *U2 by U2*, 'because now I knew what I wanted to do for the rest of my life.'

All photos taken in Canada, 1980.

Feedback's first paid gig came several months later, on Easter Monday in 1977, when they performed as part of a student-organized rock concert at St Fintan's in the northern Dublin suburbs, opening as a support act for the local pub rock bands Rat Salad and the Arthur Phybes Band. Since the Arthur Phybes Band were late, Feedback could not do a proper soundcheck. Colm O'Hare, one of the concert organizers and later a writer for *Hot Press*, recalls Larry nervously asking him if Feedback could perform second, but an argument ensued with Rat Salad who insisted on keeping the original line-up.

As well as the rushed soundcheck, Feedback had not yet worked out all their problems as a band. 'It was pretty obvious that there was a discrepancy in what you might call "musical prowess" between the band members,' said the Edge, 'but it didn't matter because we were all pretty crap.' The band struggled to finish the songs on their setlist. The Edge remembered feeling panic-stricken 20 minutes before showtime, and meeting with Larry and

Adam to discuss how to end the songs just before they were about to go onstage.

Feedback was still trying to find itself as a band. 'To say that Feedback were unrecognizable from the U2 of today would be an understatement of monumental proportions', said O'Hare in *Hot Press*. The set at St Fintan's was still all cover songs, featuring versions of 'Suffragette City', 'Nights in White Satin' and 'Johnny B. Goode'. The band was also joined by two female backup singers, Stella McCormick and Orla Dunne, who were the sisters of some friends. In *North Side Story*, Stella recalled the gig being a disaster, noting that Adam was not able to stay in time and that the sound system did not work properly, with Feedback booed off the stage by the end of their 40-minute set.

Spirits were low after the St. Fintan's gig, but not for long. Despite feeling humiliated by the concert, the rush of playing live in front of an audience was too great to ignore. Already feeling like they were outgrowing the cover songs they had been playing, the band sought to avoid the 1970s rock that dominated pubs throughout Dublin. It was music from a different generation, and they knew they needed to start making some that reflected their own if they had any chance of truly becoming a great band.

Feedback had formed in the autumn of 1976, the same year that punk rock made its way into Ireland. It was a cultural genesis for the youth of a divided nation, desperately longing for a cathartic outlet to deal with the effects of the violence of the Troubles. In Northern Ireland, where the horrors of the conflict were more common than in the south, bands like The Undertones and Stiff Little Fingers emerged with energy, power and the spirit of punk rock. For the kids who comprised these bands and their audiences, punk represented more than expressing rage brought on by the Troubles – it was an escape.

This need for escape was felt all throughout Ireland. In *U2: The Early Days*, *Hot Press* founder and U2's first champion, Bill Graham, described the nascent punk scene in Dublin as one where people were starving for rock music. 'Still innocent outsiders,' said Graham, 'they wanted to enter rock and use it to attack and extinguish the peculiar dinosaurs of their own culture's creation.' Before punk had made it over by way of the blossoming scene in the United Kingdom, Ireland's musical halls were bloated with showbands. 'Essentially electrified mutations of the post-war dance bands slimmed down … the showbands concentrated on cover versions,' said Graham. 'Beneficiaries of cultural protectionism in a land without any national or local pop stations, the showbands were the main vehicle by which the UK and American pop was disseminated in Ireland – often with hilarious and unintentionally camp ineptitude.' For the young people yearning for something more substantive, punk opened the door for Ireland to step into the modern music scene.

Punk would break for Feedback in a big way when the Ramones played their first show in Dublin in 1978. With no money or tickets, the boys sneaked into the show. 'Even though we only saw half the show, it became one of the greatest nights of our life,' said U2 in a press release promoting 2014's *Songs of Innocence* which features their tribute to the concert that changed their lives with 'The Miracle (of Joey Ramone)'. Punk's presence in

Dublin had previously only been a trickle but the Ramones had caused the dam to burst. 'I found my voice through Joey Ramone,' said Bono, '… and that was my way in.'

With the arrival of punk, Feedback were finding their voice and image within a subculture that was expanding all around them and they soon realized they needed a name to reflect that. Feedback represented an older style that no longer fitted. Borrowing from one of David Bowie's bands, the name, Feedback, was dropped in favour of The Hype, a name the band believed better captured the punk mentality.

Though punk was a huge inspiration, The Hype were not interested in being just another punk band. It was at this point, according to the Edge in *U2 by U2*, that they became serious about writing their own songs, with 'The Fool' and 'Life on a Distant Planet' being among their first. Another was 'Street Mission' which they played during their first television performance for *Youngline* on Ireland's RTÉ television network in 1978.

Just as they were beginning to find their sound as a band, tensions began to flare. While U2 would come to be known as a foursome, Feedback and the Hype had a fifth member, the Edge's brother, Dik. A few years older and already in college, Dik's schedule was making him unreliable. Without him, a natural bond started to form around the remaining members. As Dik was phased out, the group was now forced to become something new for a second time, but the question was what?

As it would turn out, the third time was the charm. Steve Averill, also known as Steve Rapid, the frontman for Ireland's first punk band The Radiators from Space, made a list of potential names for the new band, which included the Flying Tigers and the Blazers as potential marquee attractions. While the name would become one of the most recognizable and revered names in rock music, the group ultimately settled on U2 because it was cryptic and vague. Also, it was the one they disliked the least. In *U2 by U2*, Bono said he only realized the name was wordplay after U2 were drawing bigger crowds. Discussing the band's name with *TheSumOf,* Averill said that while the name evoked both a spy plane and a pun, the name was 'part of a common language' and that 'graphically speaking, a

Previous spread: Bono and Adam perform onstage at Park West, Chicago, 1981. Opposite: Larry Mullen Jnr plays during the War Tour in London, England, 1983.

single letter and a single numeral together would look very strong on a poster – it would be very identifiable.'

Now as U2, the band set out to truly make a name for themselves. In 1978, as a chance to debut under their new name, U2 entered a band contest in Limerick sponsored by Harp Lager, where the winner would be awarded £500 and a studio contract to record a demo for CBS Records Ireland. U2 watched their competition, unsure of what to expect. By the end of their three-song set, they sensed they were on to something with this new direction. They had made their debut as a band with original songs and the reaction from the audience reminded them of their first concert as Feedback at Mount Temple. 'Some bands have everything but it,' said Bono in *U2 by U2*. 'We had nothing but *it*.' Winning the contest affirmed that they did indeed have 'it'.

Jackie Hayden, the local CBS representative and one of the contest judges, recalls U2 being nervous coming into Keystone Studios to record their demo. Having very little experience as a producer, Hayden had difficulty getting them comfortable. Their musical constraints were coming through, which affected their ability to play. Until then, U2 had only played onstage or in rehearsal rooms, open spaces where they felt they could move freely. Within the controlled confines of a recording studio, with the band spread apart and limited to just the space around their microphones, their balance was off and the performance suffered for it.
'We had no idea what we were doing,' said the Edge in *U2 by U2*.

Recording at Keystone taught them they still had some things to figure out before they returned to a studio. Ahead of releasing a first single, U2 continued honing their sound by playing in clubs where they earned a reputation as a thrilling and vivacious live act. Playing nearly 50 shows throughout Dublin in 1978 as a supporting act for touring groups like XTC and The Vipers, U2 used each show as an opportunity to make an impression with their lively and spirited performance. Reviewing U2's August 1978 gig opening for Revolver at McGonagle's,

This page and following spread, Tokyo, 1983.

Hot Press's Bill Graham said, 'U2 are impressive contenders with the appetite and talent to improve beyond their already credible status,' and added that they 'profit from the fact they've an identity that needs little alteration.' One fan, in a reader's submission to *Hot Press* from July 1978, described U2's performance as rousing, with 'lead singer Hewson enticing the audience to defy the bouncers.'

Soon the right people were beginning to get a glimpse into what made U2 special. It was at the 25 May 1978 gig at the Project Arts Centre where U2 would meet their future manager Paul McGuinness. Up until then, Adam had acted as the band's manager, a role he gave himself since he was the one who called clubs throughout the week looking for gigs. A decade older than the boys in the band, Paul already had some experience in the entertainment industry, having managed a band called Spud and previously worked as a location manager for the 1974 sci-fi film *Zardoz*.

After the gig, Paul and U2 discussed the possibility of working together over drinks at McGonagle's, where the band had to be sneaked in because they were underage. In *U2 by U2*, Adam said the band wanted a manager because they felt like they were ready to play bigger venues and make a record. Paul resisted managing them for a while, believing they were not ready to take that step, but eventually came round once he felt confident about their level of commitment. In *U2 by U2*, Bono said of Paul's skill at recognizing someone's potential that he was 'never so pissed off about where things were because he knew what might be around the corner.'

With Paul as their manager, U2 soon started to play bigger gigs. They agreed to play their biggest show to date on 9 September 1978, opening for the Stranglers at the Top Hat in Dublin. It was a difficult show for the band. There was no soundcheck because they had agreed to play at short notice and the Edge broke a guitar string after only a couple of songs, resulting in rowdy hardcore punks spitting at them and flicking them with lit cigarettes. Though, according to music promoter Pat Egan, the biggest incident of the night was when U2 were confronted for stealing a bottle of wine from The Stranglers' dressing room because of how the fans treated them. It is a gig that lives

on in their memory; to this day, Larry still thanks Paul for booking it.

At the end of 1978, U2 played for 1,600 people during shows at the Stardust Club, opening for The Greedy Bastards, a supergroup made up of members from Thin Lizzy, The Boomtown Rats and The Sex Pistols. U2 were added as the support band after Bono made an agreement with Phil Lynott to play for free. It was a difficult night for U2, with *Hot Press* reviewer Neil McCormick stating he could not understand how 'a group we knew to be dynamic and inspiring could be made to sound like rank amateurs'. If they were going to become a headline act, they would have to work for it.

Going into 1979, buzz was building. In May, U2 played several afternoon concerts at the Dandelion Market, a popular local market that would become a makeshift concert venue to entice the young music lovers of Dublin into the clubs. It was there that U2 began to build their following. In a review of an August gig for *Hot Press*, Declan Lynch was amazed by the young audience saying U2 'are cooler than death and more than just another young band', becoming mentors for this new generation without even releasing a record. John Fisher, who booked gigs at the Dandelion Market, said U2 drew the biggest crowds even back then.

As they were looking to play bigger shows, U2 also strived to get a record label contract. Needing a new demo that captured their live sound which they could shop around to record executives, they returned to Keystone Studios in November 1978 to record three songs ('Street Mission', 'Shadows and Tall Trees' and 'The Fool'). In February 1979, they recorded their third demo tape, this time at Eamonn Andrews Studios where they would record six songs, three of which were later re-recorded for their 1980 debut album *Boy* ('Another Time, Another Place', 'Twilight', and 'Out of Control'). Emboldened by their new manager's support, U2 were eager to have their music heard. In *Surrender*, Bono recalls taking a trip with his girlfriend Ali to London to promote U2 among the British music press. Visiting offices for magazines like *Record Mirror*, *NME* and *Sounds*, Bono bluffed his way into meetings where he gave copies of U2's latest demo tape to the writing staff.

However, the band were getting rejections

everywhere. Though they had the reputation as one of Dublin's best live bands, U2 had difficulty transposing the energy and excitement of their concerts on to tape. Chas de Whalley, a CBS London talent scout, recalled U2's demo sounding like a 'pretty damn average post-punk band'. It was only after seeing them perform live that de Whalley began to see U2 as having potential. De Whalley was able to secure the band a two-day session at Windmill Lane Studios in Dublin to record a demo, reaching a deal that CBS could release the material as a single in Ireland without guaranteeing to sign the band if it did not meet their standards.

After two days of recording in early August in Windmill Lane, U2 released their debut record *Three* the following month, garnering much attention. Local radio DJ Dave Fanning held a contest for listeners to vote which song would become the A-side. 'Out of Control' was the winner, with 'Stories for Boys' and 'Boy/Girl' as B-sides. *Three* would become a success for U2, reaching number 19 on the Irish singles charts. In his review for *Sounds*, Dave McCullough described *Three* as a 'dazzling account of a band with amazing potential'. That potential can certainly be heard on 'Out of Control', a song U2 would return to for their debut album *Boy*. In his memoir, Bono shares that 'Out of Control' was written on his 18th birthday, inspired by the simplicity and expressiveness of 'Glad to See You Go' by the Ramones.

Excitement continued building around U2 following the release of *Three*, including them performing eight original songs for the RTÉ television special *Cork Opera House Gigs* and getting their first magazine cover with *Hot Press*. However, expectations were tempered because U2 was still without a record deal despite the recent success of *Three*.

In December 1979, after borrowing money from their parents, U2 went to London to play gigs for two weeks. This was their first time playing outside Ireland, giving them a chance to showcase not just their talent but also Ireland's place in the broader music scene. During this brief stint in London, U2 recorded their second single 'Another Day', releasing it a few months later in February.

As the calendar turned over to 1980, U2 were still no closer to a record contract. Not recognizing their uniqueness amidst all

Opposite: Performing in the Netherlands, 1981. Following spread: L-R: Record producer Steve Lillywhite, Stevie Ray Vaughan with his wife Linnie and actor Matt Dillon, New York, 1983.

the new wave and post-punk bands, labels continued to turn them down. Their demos did not capture the magic of seeing U2 play live, which was the case for Chris Blackwell, the founder of Island Records, when he saw U2 play for about a dozen people. Initially underwhelmed by their music, Blackwell was surprised by U2's tenacious personalities. 'I didn't love the music,' Blackwell told *NPR*. 'It was a little rinky-dink, but I believed in them.' It also helped that Blackwell felt that U2 had a proper manager, saying of Paul: 'He could build the band without getting in the way and dressed in a suit when very few in the music industry did. I felt these guys really had a drive and this guy was going to get them there, so I wanted to sign them.'

U2 signed their contracts with Island Records during March 1980, promising to their debut due within the first year. Since coming together nearly four years earlier, U2 had worked tirelessly to develop their own sound, one that was influenced by, but also transcended, punk rock. It took some time, with a lot of rehearsals and gigs in between, to get to a place where they could release a debut that was truly a defining opening statement for the band. Things were coming down to the wire, with their adolescence waning, but they had enough material to get started. Finishing the album would just be a matter of becoming comfortable playing in the studio without sacrificing the passion and intensity of their live sound.

Going into Windmill Lane Recording Studios to record *Boy*, nestled within Dublin's docklands, U2 had already developed a foundational philosophy after several years of playing together. The punk music scene in Dublin, according to the Edge, was starting to lose its uniqueness as musical resistance to the previous decade's boring rock had now risked becoming a fashion statement. U2 had originally approached Martin Hannett to produce the album since he had previously produced the band's earlier single '11 O'Clock Tick Tock' as well as both of Joy Division's albums *Unknown Pleasures* and *Closer*, which

U2 were fans of. Immediately, the situation in the studio was stifling. Hannett was not impressed with the facilities at Windmill Lane, so he shipped over special equipment from London at the band's expense. The band were also nervous that they would be seen as amateurs while working with a seasoned producer. Adam said they spent hours on the rhythm section developing a backing track, and Larry had difficulty keeping in time while adjusting to a new environment. However, U2's time in the studio with Hannett would be short, with Hannett departing due to the suicide of Joy Division's singer Ian Curtis. Since they had greatly admired the albums he produced for Siouxsie and the Banshees and XTC, U2 brought in Steve Lillywhite to finish producing.

The mood in the studio immediately changed with Lillywhite's arrival at Windmill Lane. Bono described Lillywhite as a breath of fresh air and Adam recalled there being a lot of excitement because the band believed they had found the right person for the job. Edge thought the sessions with Lillywhite were positive and that he had a way of working which brought out the best qualities in each of the members, even if they were still learning as musicians. Having recently produced an album for Peter Gabriel, Lillywhite introduced unconventional methods of recording sounds for *Boy*, such as smashing bottles and playing notes on bicycle wheels using forks from the studio kitchen. However, many of the tracks were based on jam sessions with musical ideas built from the riffs that resulted from these musical improvisations.

Just as the work in the studio sessions for *Boy* represented the struggle of four boys entering manhood, as musicians working to grow their talents, the final album from that journey would reveal poignant reflections about their lives and experiences along the way. The cover of *Boy* aptly captures this creative direction, which features a whitewashed and overexposed photo of a young boy. Steve Averill, who designed the cover for *Boy* and all of U2's future albums, described the image as intense and said that it 'draws you into what possibly the music could be.' Peter Rowen, the boy on the cover, was the younger brother of Derek Rowen, Bono's friend from Lypton Village who would later become the avant-garde artist Guggi and founding member of the Virgin Prunes. When they were kids, Bono and Guggi had promised each other to never grow up, so Bono wanted U2's first album 'to lay claim to the power of the naivety.' With the boy's face against white representing 'U2 in development', Bono wanted *Boy* to explore ideas absent from the rock canon like 'the end of adolescent angst, the elusiveness of being male, the sexuality, spirituality, friendship.'

'I Will Follow', the opening track on *Boy* and its second single, sets the tone for the rest of the album. From the opening count off intimating that the spirit of U2's live act is captured in the studio, it signals the coming together of four young men channelling their frustration and teenage rage. With Larry's powerful drums rising up, a glockenspiel that offers a glimmer of youthful playfulness, an urgently driven riff from the Edge and Adam's bass tying it all together while Bono recites the song's title as his opening statement, 'I Will Follow' represents both an outlet through which to express their feelings and a bold statement declaring their arrival as a band and what drives them to make music.

Bono described 'I Will Follow' as being about the unconditional love that exists between a mother and her child, adding that the lyrics could also read as a suicide note from a boy following his mother into her grave.

Childhood vulnerability is a theme woven throughout *Boy*. 'Into the Heart', segueing from 'An Cat Dubh', laments lost innocence while 'The Ocean' and 'A Day Without Me' express an angry loneliness about one's place in the world. 'Shadows and Tall Trees', 'An Cat Dubh' and 'Twilight', all songs evoking the darker side of Dublin, feature a narrator feeling restless over the unknowns of impending adulthood amidst the drama of fear and desire. 'Stories For Boys', 'Another Time, Another Place' and 'Out of Control' capture the need for escape and search for an identity. 'The Electric Co.', a song inspired by a friend's electroconvulsive therapy treatments, captures the band's emphasis on free-form

U2 circa 1981.

improvisation, conveying the intensity of a boy shouting so loud that the whole world can hear.

The themes on *Boy* are especially deep for a debut album. U2 were unlike their post-punk and new wave contemporaries whose music more often dabbled in the typical rock tropes. U2 instead wanted to capture the spirit of their own lives while also trying to make sense of it as it was changing right in front of them. While these songs conveyed complex personal and emotional ideas, the power behind these ideas came from U2's performances. As part of their creative process, U2 would put more energy into crafting the music's structure through improvisational jams before moving on to lyrics, which were often sparse and considered less important than how the song sounded. One reason, as the Edge recalled, was that U2 did not have much time to record the songs, so they wrote them quickly in order to finish the album. Though a bigger reason was that Bono did not enjoy writing lyrics because he found it difficult to concentrate on the details. Even though many of the songs for *Boy* were performed live in front of audiences before they were recorded, Bono admits that he would never learn the lyrics before going into the studio and described U2's early days as a 'non-lyric period'. 'I used to think that writing words was old fashioned,' said Bono, 'so I sketched. I wrote words on the microphone.' Even now, since their formation, U2 continue making albums by developing the musical core before developing lyrics, a process that works just as well for them as men as when they were boys.

Boy had been recorded in little over a month, with sessions finishing in September 1980, and would be the quickest U2 would ever record an album. Following its release a month later on 20 October 1980, a tour was organized to support the album, with U2 embarking on a journey through the UK before travelling to Europe to perform their first shows in the Netherlands and Belgium. The Edge recalled the tour being the first time the band had visited Europe, and they were surprised to find at their gig at the Milky Way (Melkweg) in Amsterdam that they could connect with audiences and transcend cultures despite the language barrier. On the advice from their manager that their best chance for breaking out was in America, they

played nine shows throughout the north-east thanks to support from college radio stations playing *Boy*. During their first concert in America, at a New York club called The Ritz, Larry remembers the gig not going well because Bono's anxiety affected the rest of the band. Though, by the end of their stint in America, audience reaction was generous and positive, with Larry describing their gig in Boston being so well received that it felt like a homecoming.

Boy would go on to hit number 52 on the UK album charts and number 63 on the US *Billboard* 200. The success of the album led to another tour of the UK and Europe in early 1981 in January and February, with an extensive tour across the United States and Canada following shortly from March through May. It was a modest debut that had the young band optimistic about what lay ahead.

Though when U2 returned to the studio with Lillywhite to record their second album *October*, the mood had turned an autumn grey. There was a lot of pressure to record a successful follow-up to *Boy* after the tour, which made the experience difficult for the band. Coming back from the tour with no money, Larry recalled asking a former teacher at Mount Temple to provide a

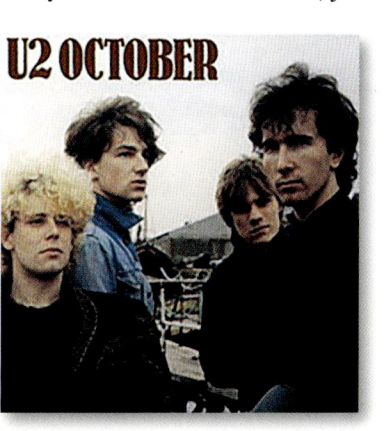

rehearsal space at the school, just as they had done a few years earlier. Adam described the experience like sticking ideas together with glue because they did not have enough time or money to focus on the music.

With the confidence they were feeling after ending their tour, the Edge assumed the songs would just naturally flow out once they rehearsed them. He believed U2 could work together quickly to develop a lot of improvised ideas, which would often include a guitar riff or drumbeat from those jam sessions, organizing the elements of a song around that. However, despite his trust that the band would form a cohesive framework for the album, the Edge said that they only ended up with pieces and fragments of musical ideas. 'We were running out of steam,' said Bono in *U2 by U2*, 'running out of enthusiasm for the world.'

There was also another reason why

recording became so stressful. Though the band felt triumphant coming back from their tour, one incident on the road would later create problems for them. On 22 March 1981, just one month before returning to the studio, Bono had lost a briefcase while performing at the Foghorn Tavern in Portland, Oregon. Inside the briefcase were scraps of paper containing lyrics and song ideas intended for their next album. Unsure of exactly how his briefcase went missing, Bono recalled being visited by two women in his dressing room. It was only after they had left that he realized his briefcase had gone missing and he frantically searched for it. The briefcase would go missing for 23 years until it was returned to Bono by two different women in 2004. Bono was relieved and called the return of his property 'an act of grace'.

However, just as was the case with *Boy*, U2 still did not put much emphasis on lyrics when recording *October*, regardless of any missing briefcase. This can be heard throughout the album, with some tracks sounding more lyrically developed than others. 'Scarlet', an instrumental track save Bono repeating 'rejoice', reveals a beautiful melody that is elevated by the lyrical sparseness. 'Is That All?' and 'Fire' offer a glimpse into U2's improvisational approach to songwriting, while 'I Fall Down' and 'Stranger in a Strange Land' feature snippets of abstract narratives.

'October', the album's title track, is a commentary on the modern world told through the stark imagery of autumn slowly chilling into winter. It had formed during a rare moment of quiet reflection during the *October* sessions, with the Edge playing a graceful piano line that made him think about a beautifully grey European setting. Bono then added the lyrics of bare trees and falling leaves to describe the cultural and economic bleakness felt during the 1980s.

Some themes from *Boy* also return for *October*. Anxiety and self-confidence resurface in 'I Threw a Brick Through a Window', a song Bono says is really about smashing your mirror's reflection. 'Tomorrow', featuring Irish uilleann pipes, is about Bono grieving his mother. With such a tight schedule to finish the album, these themes were still fresh for U2 to work into songs.

The pressure followed them even outside the studio. While recording *October*, U2 were invited to open for Thin Lizzy at Slane Castle. Slane Castle was the biggest open-air concert venue in Ireland at that time, but U2 decided they were going to perform their new songs despite never having played them together as a band outside the studio. Due to their inexperience with the material, as well as some equipment issues, Bono and the Edge agree that it was one of U2's biggest concert failures.

The band were also struggling with personal difficulties. Bono, the Edge and Larry, though not Adam, were still active in the religious group Shalom, an evangelical Christian community where people shared living space and responsibilities in accordance with strict biblical teachings. Bono recalled his early experiences studying Scripture with Shalom as amazing, but soon they were pressured to make a decision about their lives. Other members in Shalom were demanding that U2 quit making music and instead fully dedicate themselves to Christianity, which created turmoil within the band.

Shalom were so forceful that the strain almost caused U2 to break up. It was such a difficult time for the band, the Edge recalled, as they struggled to balance the demands of their spirituality and musical aspirations, that he briefly quit U2. In his memoir, Bono recalls supporting his friend's decision to quit the band. When Bono visited the Edge at his parents' home, the Edge told Bono, 'I've got a problem I can't solve in U2. I'm not sure I want to make music this way.' The Edge felt Shalom were demanding he answer questions he did not even understand, making him wonder whether U2 could 'be a band of believers'. Bono understood the Edge, as he was troubled by this same issue, but offered his perspective saying, 'There's a special feeling when we play. It's when we stop playing I feel like shit'.

In *Surrender*, Bono shares how U2 survived nearly coming to a premature end after their manager Paul convinced them to stay together. When the band met with their manager to discuss them breaking up U2 for religious reasons, Paul said, 'Well, maybe next time you might ask God if it's okay for your representative on earth to break a legal contract.' Seeing the boys were confused by his response, Paul continued asking them whether God would approve of them not fulfilling their contractual obligations. This was based on the idea that God did not want them to break the law in which U2 remained a band.

U2's religious convictions can be heard throughout *October*. This theme is captured in the lyrics of multiple songs, with 'With a Shout (Jerusalem)' and 'Rejoice' being two of the more overtly devout tracks on the album.

'Gloria', the album's opening track, stands out as being one of their best spiritual works. When panic began to set in because the band were short on lyrics, the Edge says ideas started to form out of desperation. Inspired by Van Morrison's song recorded with Them, as well as a Gregorian chant album given to them by their manager, 'Gloria', with its signature Latin chorus, becomes Bono searching for the words to express U2's spiritual feelings. Before this, faith had forced limitations on what they could achieve as a band, but it was now helping them forge their musical path.

October was released in 1981 on the 12th of that month, peaking at number 11 on the UK charts but not selling as well as *Boy*. The album earned mixed reviews and little radio support, though the band would realize years later that *October* was better than they initially thought. *October*'s chilly reception served as an omen right as U2 were about to go out on tour to support it. With little cash or support from their record company, the band did their best to bring *October* to audiences until their manager reached the limit on his credit card and could no longer finance the tour. If U2 had been signed with another label, Paul believes they would have been dropped.

Recording *October* was an experience that truly tested the spirit and will of U2, but they still had some drive and motivation to give their dreams another shot. The battle lines were being redrawn, with the only options being either to surrender or continue fighting to have their music heard. With one last chance to see just how far they could go as a band, U2 went to war for their own survival.

As soon as the October Tour ended, they

immediately began developing ideas for a new album. The band rented a beachside house on Dublin's Northside in Howth where they could live together and collaborate in a makeshift rehearsal space in one of the rooms. Accordingto Larry, the house was where the band could focus on developing songs that could become more refined than their earlier work. Adam recalls U2 wanting their third album to have a more abrasive sound that created a more fierce and ambitious experience for the listener. Bono said he wanted the new album to have a rougher sonic texture compared to *Boy* and *October* and even considered using a different producer for each song to vary the album's sonic flow.

War, as an album promising a distinctly more aggressive-sounding U2, was released on 28 February 1983, becoming U2's first career-defining album with music and messaging that continues to resonate with listeners and audiences today. As U2's breakthrough album, *War* is filled with passion and bombast that showcases their sharpened musical skills as well as the core of their sound and identity as a band. The Edge says *War* is a reactionary response to mainstream pop he believed had no character. With the band spending more time on song development, *War* represented a bolder and more assertive U2, distancing the band from assumptions based on what they had done before.

Though still rooted in post-punk like its predecessors, several tracks on *War* demonstrate U2 reaching for newer styles and sounds. Irish musician Steve Wickham helped expand the sonic scope of the album, providing electric violin on 'Sunday Bloody Sunday' and 'Drowning Man'. Kid Creole and the Coconuts backed U2 on 'Surrender' and 'Red Light', the latter featuring a stellar trumpet performance from Kenny Fradley that spiced up the track. *War* also features several songs that reveal the more personal aspects of the album, while still broadening the album musically. 'Two Hearts Beat as One' was written while Bono was on his honeymoon,

and would spawn several dance remixes that brought U2's sound into the clubs, while 'Like a Song…' was Bono responding to the vapidness of U2's punk critics.

However, one of the most revered songs on *War*, and among the most beloved in all of U2's catalogue, is '40'. Reimagined from the Bible's Psalm 40, the song earned its legacy as a concert closer with the audience singing the refrain while U2 quietly left the stage. During a 1987 concert, Bono said '40' was recorded just before the band were kicked out of the studio for going over their allotted time. Bono, the Edge and Larry were still in the studio refining a song idea that the Edge had previously worked on with no success. Bono read from the Bible, with Lillywhite mixing his vocals with the guitar and bass tracks the Edge was laying down. As soon as the vocals were mixed, the band left and *War* had finally been recorded.

Even the visual design of *War* makes a statement about U2's creative direction, such as the band's name and album title appearing in bold, red type. 'It's a heavy title …' said the Edge, 'but we wanted to take a more dangerous course … so I think the title is appropriate. The last two albums have both had a key to the songs in the title and this one's no different. Not all the songs are about war, but it's a good general heading. It's a big step forward for us, because we're laying ourselves on the line …' Peter Rowen, the boy whose visage graced *Boy*, returns with a battle-scarred intensity that created an iconic image which furthered the impact of *War*. 'Instead of putting tanks and guns on the cover, we've put a child's face,' said Bono. 'War can also be a mental thing, an emotional thing between loves. It doesn't have to be a physical thing.' Juxtaposed with *Boy*, the image of *War* is that of an innocence lost.

War was also U2's declaration that they were a band with something more to say, beginning their legacy that infused rock with political and social consciousness. 'The Refugee', the only track on *War* produced by Bill Whelan, is the story of a young woman yearning for freedom in America and for her

Bono climbing the stage at a performance in Belgium, 1982.

husband to return from a war they do not understand. Featuring lead vocal contributions from the Edge, 'Seconds' expresses Bono's fear at the ease with which madmen can create nuclear weapons in cities.

War also contains two songs that not only introduced U2's political messaging to wider audiences but have since become among the most beloved songs in their catalogue. 'New Year's Day' was inspired by the Polish Solidarity movement and other global conflicts that had recently emerged. Though it initially began as a love song by Bono for his wife Ali, the final version of 'New Year's Day' originated from a soundcheck jam where the band were connecting the song's signature piano with the melody. The song debuted in the UK's top 10 before hitting the top of the UK charts after War was released. Since its release, it has become one of U2's most well-known hits and a beloved concert staple and earned accolades as being one of the greatest songs of all time according to Rolling Stone. The lyrics sound relevant and modern as Bono offers the cold, hard truth that the world's problems will continue even though we try to forget them.

However, War's defining track is its opener. Centred on the 1972 Bloody Sunday incident in Derry, in which British soldiers shot and killed over two dozen unarmed civilians during a protest march, 'Sunday Bloody Sunday' would come to transcend that moment and become U2's lasting statement condemning state violence and oppression. With a militaristic drumbeat and savagely ruthless guitar, U2 asks the rhetorical question: what is the point of all the senseless violence in the world? With a subtext that is only matched by 'New Year's Day' on the album, Bono sings that closing our eyes will not make the bloodshed cease and disappear.

The initial structure of 'Sunday Bloody Sunday' came from the Edge channelling his frustration and depressed feelings into music until he realized he had inadvertently begun writing an anti-terrorism song. Bono then later connected the song's core idea with Bloody Sunday. The ramifications of this decision were deep since the Republic of Ireland and Northern Ireland were still in the midst of an ethno-nationalist conflict called the Troubles, and there was some fear that 'Sunday Bloody Sunday' could incite violence.

Performing on *The Tube*, 1983.

The Edge recalled a show in Belfast after recording *War* where Bono, unbeknownst to the others, told the audience that if they did not like the song they were about to play, which was 'Sunday Bloody Sunday', they would never play it again. The audience loved it.

A bold gamble on which to bet what would become a classic song, that performance of 'Sunday Bloody Sunday' would be overshadowed by one that would not only expand upon the song's legacy and power but also signal U2's breakthrough in America. The performance of the song that appears on *Under a Blood Red Sky*, U2's live EP recorded during the War Tour, opens with Bono clarifying what the song meant. As a protest against its appropriation as a rallying song in support of sectarian violence, Bono clears the air once and for all, declaring 'Sunday Bloody Sunday' is not a rebel song.

Accompanying the EP was the concert film *U2 Live at Red Rocks: Under a Blood Red Sky*, recorded live on 5 June 1983, at the Red Rocks Amphitheatre in Colorado, USA, with songs from the concert being broadcast on Showtime and MTV. U2 had wanted to play Red Rocks because the rock formations that the amphitheatre was built into were stunning, so they spent the last of their funds to produce the film, but the concert that would become a landmark moment in U2's history almost did not happen because of rain. There was already too much water onstage and another storm was expected. Adam recalls the concert promoter claiming on the radio the concert would be cancelled, so U2 did interviews encouraging people to still come. Fortunately, the rain cleared away two hours before U2 were scheduled to play, but the prior threat of rain meant that only 2,000 attended the 7,000-capacity venue. However, since the film was shot using wide-angle lenses, U2 look like they are performing to a packed house, with the wet mist creating a crimson haze that makes the whole show appear other-worldly.

U2's performance of 'Sunday Bloody Sunday' was repackaged for a music video which helped build their reputation as a thrilling live act for those watching at home. Bono waving a white flag personified the intensity and spirit of the music, an iconic image that announced the band's arrival. The EP and film were successful and the video secured a legacy as one of the great moments in rock history.

With three albums that traced their journey from the suburbs of Dublin to the airwaves of America, U2 had exceeded expectations of what they could accomplish together as four friends making music. They had developed a sound through punk rock and found a way to imbue that spirit with their own changing identity. This period of U2's career is important because it marks the early days when they shaped their ethos as artists. It created a spirit that is deeply connected to a time and place that inspired their most raw and unabashed music.

With new-found success and audiences came an opportunity for U2 to find fresh inspiration that would expand them creatively and challenge what they had learned so far. They had come a long way from Dublin, but their musical journey was only just beginning. The future looked bright for U2, but it was a matter of taking a spark and building a fire.

Adam Clayton,
London, 1983.

2

In God's Country

The start of 1984 signalled a change in U2's sound

. While *Boy*, *October* and *War* had their own distinct qualities as individual works of musical art, they were still rooted in post-punk. U2 did not want to copy what they had already done before. 'We didn't want to be the same…' said the Edge. 'After *War*, our fan base clearly grew and they weren't the same ones from the beginning. We had the opportunity to speak to others, to show who we were to a larger audience. And we were much more than we had shown them until then.'

War reflected a harder rock sound than when U2 first entered the studio several years earlier, but now they were searching for another feeling. In *U2 by U2*, Adam recalls wanting their music to be more artistically serious. Thinking about bands they enjoyed that could possibly ignite their inspiration, Roxy Music kept coming up during their discussions. Their sound blended progressive art rock with sophisticated pop atmospherics that created a distinctly musical European sensibility that U2 found intriguing. The band approached Rhett Davies, who had produced both Roxy Music's 1980 album *Flesh + Blood* as well as their acclaimed 1982 follow-up *Avalon*, but nothing came from their meeting. Still, Roxy Music remained on their minds. Eventually, U2 thought to ask the band's former keyboard player Brian Eno.

U2 were certainly interested in working with Eno, but the feeling was not mutual at first. Eno had produced albums by artists that had huge influences on U2, like Talking Heads, but he was not drawn to the band. When Bono called Eno to discuss producing U2's next album, Eno said he planned to retire because he was bored producing rock albums and wanted to focus more on visual art. Bono told him that after three albums, U2 were more comfortable working in a studio, and were eager to make their new album in an actual place, rejecting the confinement of a studio in favour of a space that allowed them to develop a new sound more naturally. U2's desire to work outside a studio interested Eno enough for him to book a flight to Dublin to meet with them.

During their lunch meeting, Eno told U2 that he did not plan to produce their album and only kept the meeting because he had agreed to it. Eno also had a different motive for meeting. He

Previous page: Bono, Los Angeles, 1984. Opposite: The Edge in Sydney, 1984.

had decided to bring along Daniel Lanois, an engineer who had worked with him on his recent albums, 1982's *Ambient 4: On Land* and 1983's *Apollo: Atmospheres and Soundtracks*. According to the Edge in *U2 by U2*, Lanois was interested in producing U2's next album so the meeting became an opportunity for Eno to introduce an experienced engineer he knew could do an excellent job. However, the band kept imploring Eno to produce the album despite his disinterest, discussing with him their ideas for capturing the essence of their performance within a room's natural ambience. This persistence paid off, eventually convincing Eno that the vision for their music was more interesting than he initially thought. 'I told Bono the final result would be very different from U2's previous records, that it would be unrecognizable and people might not understand...' said Eno. 'They accepted and everything took off.'

In their search for the best place to record their fourth album, U2 toured Slane Castle, located an hour north of Dublin. Built in the 1780s by the Conyngham family following the Battle of the Boyne, the castle began hosting rock festivals in 1981 in the grounds' amphitheatre. Slane Castle was also notable for its high-domed neo-Gothic ballroom. Impressed with the natural acoustics of the ballroom, U2 decided Slane Castle was the environment they needed for their ambient aspirations. With Eno and Lanois at the production helm, U2 turned the castle into a makeshift studio, relying on the ballroom for its sonic atmosphere and with recording done in the library due to its superior acoustic quality. At Slane Castle, the Edge said U2 could 'try and take what would be a wild sound' instead of trying to create a facsimile in a studio.

The dynamic between the band and the producers became apparent early on in the recording process. Eno was bringing U2 exactly what they had asked for: grand artistic ideas that transcended ordinary rock 'n' roll and pushed them into uncharted territory. They were eager to do that, but they also did not want to lose themselves along the way. Disagreements broke out between U2 and Eno, recalled the Edge in *U2 by U2*, with Eno apathetic towards ideas that disinterested him. However, they did find common ground as both U2 and Eno preferred to develop song

ideas by experimenting with improvisational jams. Eno would sometimes experiment on a synthesizer and encourage U2 to play over it. Improvised exercises like these encouraged the band to approach the music more organically and without restraint.

Lanois, offering an alternative musical perspective, brought in the rock element to balance out his avant-garde production colleague. Working closely with U2, Lanois connected with them to better understand how they worked as a band in order to make the songwriting process less complicated, often encouraging them to try something different if an idea was not working out. 'My technical abilities were limited,' said Larry, 'but my desire to experiment was enormous. Eno and Lanois gave me total freedom; I didn't have to simply keep the time, but I could free my creativity and find increasingly better results along with them.'

'With Steve [Lillywhite], we were a lot stricter about a song and what it should be,' said Adam. 'If it did veer off to the left or the right, we would pull it back as opposed to chasing it. Brian and Danny were definitely interested in watching where a song went and then chasing it.'

Speaking with *Pitchfork* in 2009, Eno said he wanted to work on the album's musical ideas while Lanois would work with the band to translate them into the production, saying, 'I had never worked with that kind of music before, and I was not completely convinced that I would be the right person for it ... I knew Dan was very good at that side of things, and very good at working with bands, getting the best out of the players and so on, so I said, "Why not have both of us? We'll sort of overlap in some parts, but we actually sort of serve different functions as well."'

U2 had always been open to experimentation, but sometimes situations would get tense during recording because of some of the band's old habits. In *U2 by U2*, Adam says that U2's inability to take musical ideas and turn them into complete songs sometimes resulted in a strained atmosphere. As with earlier albums, Bono paid less attention to writing lyrics than he did with performing those lyrics. This was encouraged by Eno and Lanois who wanted the lyrics to be little more than rough outlines, but according to Larry in *U2 by U2*, Bono had to be

British musician and composer Brian Eno.

constantly singing in order to finish a song, which would affect the band's performance depending on whether he was in the room or singing from elsewhere. 'I think we did the best we could with what we had to work with. We had very few tools, and there were no outside influences. We were huddled up as a team, and we got what we got because of what we brought to the table,' said Lanois to *Pitchfork* in 2009.

'With Eno we discovered the spirit of our music and a confidence in ourselves,' said Bono. 'The emphasis was on the moment in recording, on the spontaneity.'

Released on 1 October 1984, just two months after they finished recording, *The Unforgettable Fire* revealed a new U2. The title was inspired by an exhibition held at the former Peace Museum in Chicago, which highlighted visual art created by survivors of the atomic bombings in Hiroshima and Nagasaki by the United States. The turning towards art to process the trauma of nuclear holocaust left a major impression on the band. 'Painting was a part of the therapy to help these people purge themselves of their internal emotions,' said the Edge. 'Later we found the title fit the new record in many ways, especially in reflecting its multicoloured textures.'

Due to the ambient experimental process making of *The Unforgettable Fire*, as well as the band finding it difficult to finish songs, the album is more impressionistic than U2's earlier work. The album's title track eschews a direct commentary on that historical atrocity for an emotional and blurry collage of lyrical images. Bono describes the lyrics for 'The Unforgettable Fire' as a sketch that 'builds up a picture' but 'doesn't tell you anything'. While *The Unforgettable Fire* as an album was not directly about that horror, the idea that art can heal resonated with the album's underlying motif.

Many of the songs are fragments of ideas. 'Wire' conveys complex feelings on heroin abuse, an issue that was exploding in Dublin. 'A Sort of Homecoming', borrowing from poet Paul Celan who said, 'Poetry is a sort of homecoming', reflects Bono exploration of lyrical influences through his insatiable appetite for reading. Trying to capture what Bono described as a 'sense of spirit in a concrete jungle' and 'wanting to break through a city to an open place', 'Indian Summer Sky' reveals the cinematic nature of the album and how quickly lyrics were sketched to capture that.

Other tracks on *The Unforgettable Fire* highlight the album's experimental qualities. Eno was known for his Oblique Strategies, a series of cards co-developed with multimedia artist Peter Schmidt and designed to stimulate creative impulses, which included suggestions such as using old ideas or working at different speeds. 'Promenade' features stream of consciousness style lyrics that helped Bono become more relaxed as a singer, while '4th of July' came from an unrehearsed instrumental that had been secretly recorded by Lanois. Perhaps the most unconventional track on the album is 'Elvis Presley and America' which features Bono improvising lyrics while listening to a slowed down instrumental version of 'A Sort of Homecoming' for the first time. According to the Edge, Eno insisted that vocals be recorded in a single take to preserve the continuity of the performance. Bono said, 'When I picked up the mic it was a completely off-the-wall thing and I just began to sing.'

Though a departure from their earlier work, *The Unforgettable Fire* did include what would become one of U2's most memorable songs and a hit that signalled the band was on the right path with their new creative direction. 'Pride (In the Name of Love)' was born out of a soundcheck as U2 practised some chord changes. After American journalist Jim Henke gave Bono a copy of Stephen B. Oates's book *Let the Trumpet Sound: A Life of Martin Luther King, Jr* and a Malcolm X biography, he became interested in the contrast between the violent and peaceful sides of the civil rights movement. 'Pride (In the Name of Love)' became U2's first top 40 hit in the United States, with its popularity enduring as U2's second most played song live

Larry Mullen Jnr playing during the Lovetown Tour in Dublin, 1989. Following spread: L-R: George Michael, promoter Harvey Goldsmith, Bono, Paul McCartney and Freddie Mercury performing on stage during the finale of Live Aid, London, 1985.

after 'Sunday Bloody Sunday'. U2 returned
to the essence of Dr King again on 'MLK', a
spiritual lullaby that closes the album just as
'40' did with *War*.

'Bad', another song inspired by Dublin's
heroin epidemic, is Bono contemplating his
own vulnerability and fear of temptation.
With the pressures of recording at Slane
Castle, Bono felt 'Bad' was unfinished and had
a lot more potential, describing it in *U2 by U2*
as a 'huge promise of a song'.

Though not released as a single, 'Bad' has
an enduring legacy beyond *The Unforgettable
Fire*. In May 1985, U2 released their *Wide
Awake in America* EP, which featured two
B-sides, 'The Three Sunrises' and 'Love Comes
Tumbling', as well as live versions of 'A Sort
of Homecoming' and 'Bad'. 'Bad' quickly
became a fan favourite during concerts, with
the EP version cracking the rock charts in
the United States thanks to heavy airplay on
album-oriented stations. Performing 'Bad'
for audiences, Bono said it gave him the
opportunity to finish it by treating the song as
a living thing that can be revised.

It was during a live performance of 'Bad'
that U2's career would blossom in front of a
worldwide audience. On 13 July 1985, along
with two dozen other artists like Queen and
David Bowie, U2 performed at London's
Wembley Stadium as part of a global benefit
concert called Live Aid. Organized by Midge
Ure and Bob Geldof, the latter of whom had
come out of the Dublin music scene with
The Boomtown Rats, Live Aid raised funds
to provide food relief for famine-ravaged
Ethiopia. Over 72,000 people packed into
Wembley, with another 89,000 attending the
concert's American counterpart at John F.
Kennedy Stadium in Philadelphia, connected
via satellite links and broadcast to 1.9 billion
people across 150 countries.

U2 were scheduled to play a three-song set,
consisting of 'Sunday Bloody Sunday' followed
by 'Bad' and then 'Pride (In the Name of
Love)', but things didn't go as planned.
During 'Bad', Bono saw a young woman being
crushed against the barrier by the audience
and desperately trying to get help. Bono
tried to alert security but they could not
hear him, so he jumped offstage to help pull
her from the throng. The two then shared
a dance. Not aware of what was happening
but still annoyed by what appeared to be

Bono and Adam Clayton,
Chicago, 1985.
Following spread: At the
Milk Music Awards in the
National Concert Hall.
L-R Adam Clayton, Bob
Geldof and Bono. U2 won
Best International Group,
Best Irish Group and
Best Irish Album for *The
Unforgettable Fire*.

egotistical frontman showboating, the rest of the band continued to play 'Bad', which had already been extended with snippets of 'Ruby Tuesday' by The Rolling Stones and Lou Reed's 'Satellite of Love' and 'Walk on the Wild Side'. This version of 'Bad' clocked in at 12 minutes and forced them to cut 'Pride (In the Name of Love)' from the set which had been their biggest hit to date, resulting in an argument among the band backstage afterwards.

U2's set at Live Aid had been the closer for The Unforgettable Fire Tour. A year earlier, before the album was even released, U2 embarked on their first tour of Australia and New Zealand where they debuted several songs from *The Unforgettable Fire* as part of a setlist that still resembled the War Tour. Those shows made them realize they needed to practise the new songs more, forcing them to cancel concerts and delaying the next leg of the tour in Europe that coincided with the album's release. As U2 played throughout Europe and America, their concerts soon began to reflect the atmospheric mood of *The Unforgettable Fire*, connecting earlier songs with their new musical direction.

The Unforgettable Fire was well received by critics and did well on the charts, topping the UK albums chart and peaking at number 12 on the US *Billboard* 200, but it was U2's audiences that truly measured how far the band had come. On 29 June 1984, U2 played their first stadium headlining show during a homecoming concert at Dublin's Croke Park. By the tour's fifth leg, U2 were now exclusively playing arenas throughout the United States and Canada. As their audience grew, it was clear that U2 were on the cusp of global fame and success. They just needed one more push to get them over that threshold towards widespread acclaim. U2 viewed Live Aid as the right moment to make that happen, but they left the stage thinking they had failed. 'We felt like we'd blown an opportunity to be great,' Larry said.

They would not realize it until later, but audiences throughout the world were enamoured by U2's performance at Live Aid. Looking back at their performance, the Edge said in *U2 by U2*, 'It really took us by surprise when people started talking about U2 as one of the noteworthy performances of the day. I thought they were joking; I really thought we were crap. But looking back, as I did a

35A   36   36

week later, I started to see what it was. It was the sense of real, total jeopardy, which is always very exciting for a live event, and Bono's complete determination to make physical contact with the crowd and eventually getting there after two minutes of struggling over barriers. I think there was something about the effort he had to put in to do it that somehow made it even more powerful.'

U2's platform was growing, and with more ears to listen than ever before. In March 1985, only halfway through the decade, *Rolling Stone* called U2 the 'Band of the '80s', saying they had 'become the band that matters most, maybe even the only band that matters'. Now that they were getting people's attention, they could use their voice to motivate real change.

On 17 May 1986, U2 performed at Self Aid, a benefit concert that pledged to resolve Dublin's rising unemployment crisis. The largest concert held in Ireland at that time, it included a line-up of Irish artists including Clannad, Rory Gallagher, The Pogues and more. As U2 were becoming a much bigger band, Self Aid was a sort of homecoming that showed their music could be used for good.

During June 1986, U2 also took part in the A Conspiracy of Hope Tour alongside other artists such as Peter Gabriel, Lou Reed, The Neville Brothers, and also a reunion by The Police. Instead of raising money, the series of six concerts in the United States was held to raise public awareness over the human rights work that Amnesty International had been doing for 25 years. U2's sets largely featured their most political songs, such as 'Sunday Bloody Sunday' and 'Pride (In the Name of Love)', as well as covers with their messaging meant to inspire people to act such as The Beatles' 'Help!' and 'Maggie's Farm' and 'I Shall Be Released' by Bob Dylan.

As part of their encore during the A Conspiracy of Hope Tour, U2 also performed 'Sun City', a 1985 protest song written by Steven Van Zandt to oppose government apartheid policies in South Africa. Featuring a stellar line-up of over 50 artists, including Bruce Springsteen, Herbie

Stills from U2's performance at Live Aid, London 1985.

37 37A 38

Hancock, Darlene Love, Bonnie Raitt, Gil Scott-Heron, Miles Davis, Afrika Bambaataa and more recording under the collective name Artists United Against Apartheid, 'Sun City' was a protest by the music industry against performing at the Sun City resort casino, which was built by forcing indigenous South Africans off their land. Bono participated on 'Sun City' and also contributed the track 'Silver and Gold' to the album which featured guitar by The Rolling Stones' Keith Richards and Ronnie Wood.

Not long after U2's performance at Live Aid, Bono was invited by the humanitarian organization World Vision to witness first-hand the famine ravaging Ethiopia. Bono had previously participated in the star-studded charity single 'Do They Know It's Christmas?', released in December 1984 under the name Band Aid. Like Live Aid, this was also organized by Bob Geldof to raise funds for famine relief in Ethiopia. Now that Live Aid had broken U2 to a wider audience and furthered their journey towards rock stardom, Bono was careful that his humanitarian work should not become another celebrity public-relations stunt. When finally assured that World Vision was serious in their mission, Bono and his wife Ali left to secretly spend a month working in orphanages and relief camps in northern Ethiopia, where they provided food and aid to refugees as well as taught basic hygiene to children through songs. Steve Reynolds, the communications director for World Vision at that time, recalls taking Bono on tours of the camps, saying, 'Something in him had changed. As we walked through row after row of makeshift huts and shelters where people waited for the next food handout, Bono showed tireless compassion. It seemed he wanted to hold every child and comfort every mother.'

With these humanitarian causes, Bono recognized the power that music could have as a positive force for change in the world. In *U2 by U2*, Bono said, 'Music was now seen as a unifying force, a kind of glue to make a new political constituency.' His interest in human rights advocacy would soon grow in a way that would follow him into the studio. 'I felt the time had come to write words that meant something, out of my experience,' said Bono.

Following the success of *The Unforgettable Fire*, U2 teamed up again with Eno and Lanois to produce their next album. U2 wanted to expand their sonic atmosphere but forgo ambient experimentation in favour of a more defined musical vision. Focusing on 'the primary colours of rock 'n' roll' – guitar, bass and drums – the Edge said for their next album 'that maybe options were not a good thing, that limitations might be positive. And so we decided to work within the limitations of the song as a starting point. We thought, *let's actually write songs*. We wanted the record to be less vague, open-ended, atmospheric and impressionistic. To make it more straightforward, focused and concise.' Unlike their approach to recording *The Unforgettable Fire*, Lanois encouraged U2 to develop ideas for their music before recording in the studio to inspire a more thematic cohesiveness.

In the spirit of crafting a more concise and refined sound, the band and production crew decided not to return to Slane Castle. Instead, they created studio spaces inside two houses: Danesmoate, a large Georgian house outside Dublin in the foothills of the Wicklow Mountains – bought two years later in 1988 by Adam Clayton – and a seaside house called Melbeach that the Edge had recently purchased. As the band and production crew were already familiar with each other's working styles, the mood during these sessions was lighter and more easygoing when recording began in January 1986.

This notion that music can drive political change planted a seed within U2, with them sensing a growing feeling that they needed to become a band with something important to say. The first step then became to concentrate on songwriting. Previously, U2 tended to create musical ideas together. With a new focus on songwriting, the band dynamic would shift, with Bono and the Edge forming a song's foundations before bringing it to Adam and Larry. 'We approached arranging and producing each song like it was unique. We just hoped the album would have a sonic cohesiveness based on the idea that we were playing it,' said the Edge.

While touring, U2 became entranced by the landscape of the American desert. Adam described the desert as a blank canvas, saying that it represented a wasteland for some but also a source of positive imagery if seen from a certain point of view. 'The desert was intensely inspirational to us as a

mental image,' said Adam. Bono echoed this sentiment, saying, 'Even though the mood of a lot of songs is very bleak, there is also a feeling of pure joy in there.'

Their sojourn also opened doors within themselves, affecting their view of their relationship with America. 'It's all relative to our interest in America,' said the Edge. 'It's like we really didn't discover our Irishness until we travelled out of Ireland then you go to America and you find yourself totally alienated by it. Then, slowly, you realize there are different levels to it.' This personal revelation followed them into the studio. 'We wanted to give each song a sense of location,' said Larry.

As much as America fascinated them, they became aware of the darker elements hidden beneath the surface. However, instead of turning away, they scratched at the façade. What they found through their experience would provide them with a more complex understanding of America, one that conflicted with their belief that it was a promised land. Torn between loving and hating the country, Bono said, 'I have two conflicting visions of America: one is a kind of dream landscape and the other is a kind of black comedy.'

They were finding out that not only was the American dream not real, but that it had become a nightmare for many people. Growing up in Ireland, a country whose people historically endured famine and political turmoil, U2 had come to see the idea of America as a symbol of hope. It took them travelling to America, and seeing it up close, to understand the image of America they had believed in was an apocryphal one. 'There's two Americas; there's the mythic America and the real America,' Bono told *NPR*. 'We were obsessed by America at the time. America's a sort of promised land for Irish people – and then, a sort of potentially broken promised land.'

In response to this revelation, U2's new album was originally to be called *The Two Americas*, their critique of the country that had opened their arms to an up-and-coming rock band. The artistic direction for the album art was to capture the point where the desert collided with civilization, with the yucca palms providing a stark contrast to the imagery of their previous albums. Steve Averill, the album designer, told U2 about the

Bono in Australia during The Unforgettable Fire Tour, 1984.

legend of the yucca palms scattered across the desert, saying they were called Joshua trees by early Mormon settlers because the branches resembled hands raised towards the heavens in prayer. The next morning, Bono suggested the album should be called *The Joshua Tree*.

U2's recent experiences and understanding of America would directly impact their songwriting. During the album recording sessions in July 1986, Bono travelled to El Salvador and Nicaragua to see the impact of the United States president Ronald Reagan's foreign policies in Central America. The Reagan administration, as part of a Cold War initiative to suppress communism, provided support through military equipment and funding to the regimes that seized government power through *coup d'état*. Reagan continued to support these regimes even after they oppressed revolutionary uprisings that resulted in them committing human rights atrocities against their citizens which included forced disappearances, torture and extrajudicial killings. There, Bono witnessed the extreme poverty that was rampant throughout the region, largely stemming from an economic blockade enforced by the United States. He also saw the extent to which the government used the military to subdue its citizens and was even shot at himself by government soldiers while delivering aid. Recalling his experience, Bono told *NPR*, 'We witnessed a firebombing in rebel-backed territory, watching people's livelihoods get exploded and feeling the ground shake, even though we were safe enough ourselves. It was something that made, as you can imagine, a bit of an impression: Seeing bodies thrown out of cars on the side of the road, terrible stuff that was going on. Watching foreign policy work itself out in a small country.'

The devastation left an indelible impression on Bono, one he wanted to emotionally channel into music. Returning to the studio, Bono asked the Edge 'to put El Salvador through an amplifier,' creating the feedback distortion that would become 'Bullet the Blue Sky'. As U2's most overtly political song up to that point, and arguably to date, it signalled a new direction for the band in which they expressed social and cultural commentary through music. 'When I

explained to Edge what I'd been through in El Salvador,' said Bono for the Rock & Roll Hall of Fame's Louder Than Words: Rock, Power & Politics exhibit, 'he was able to … try and put some of that fear and loathing into his guitar solo.'

While U2 had previously blended politics with their music for earlier songs such as 'Sunday Bloody Sunday' and 'New Year's Day', the messaging within those songs was much broader. With 'Bullet the Blue Sky', U2 were addressing issues that were currently happening. With lyrics evoking the violence he saw delivered with a haunting, howling vocal to match its intensity, Bono brought a new-found urgency and relevance to U2's music and songwriting. 'As a student of non-violence,' said Bono for Louder Than Words, '… I was having a violent reaction to what I was witnessing.'

Bono also met with members of COMADRES while in El Salvador, an organization of mothers demanding accountability from their government over the disappearances and murders of their family, after being made aware of their struggle earlier. After U2's performance on the first night of the A Conspiracy of Hope Tour in Daly City, California, Bono met René Castro, a Chilean artist exiled after two years of torture in a concentration camp, known for his flat-style mural paintings protesting against dictator Augusto Pinochet. It was through Castro's art and friendship that Bono learned about the work of COMADRES and the Madres de Plaza de Mayo, another activist group whose children were forcibly disappeared by the dictatorships in Argentina and Chile.

This concerted effort to silence people demanding their human rights motivated Bono to write 'Mothers of the Disappeared', a lament conveying the unimaginable heartbreak these mothers endure. As with 'Bullet the Blue Sky', 'Mothers of the Disappeared' is a condemnation of the United States' role in such cruelty. Bono said in the December 1986 issue of *Propaganda*, 'There's no question in my mind of the Reagan administration's involvement in backing the regime that is committing these atrocities.'

As Bono saw it, the people in Central and South America were advocating for their freedom and basic human rights, with Reagan preaching compassionate values to voters back in the United States while also remaining complicit towards the inhumanity that silenced voices in other countries. Whether they were apathetic to what was happening or merely unaware, Bono believed Americans were tricked into trusting 'a man as dangerous as Ronald Reagan.' 'People were so behind everything Ronald Reagan stood for,' said the Edge, 'but now I think when we go back to America we'll see a broken country. Either that or people refusing to look – which is a more frightening prospect.'

However, U2 would find that America's hypocrisy did not just affect people outside its border but also the lives of its own citizens. With allusions to the Statue of Liberty as a desert rose, whose beauty is graced with prickly thorns, 'In God's Country' reveals the vain hope that the people in the American heartland have despite being left behind by their leaders. Bono sings of them as dreamers waiting to see the golden fortune that awaits them beyond the reach of their own meagre existence, but instead they are burned by the fire of America's false promises.

Straying further into the country's darkest impulses, 'Exit' is the story of a man giving himself over to violence after being denied the American dream. Bono had become fascinated with American literature, especially the New Journalism movement which blended traditional journalism with non-fiction narrative storytelling. Inspired by works such as Norman Mailer's *The Executioner's Song* and Truman Capote's *In Cold Blood*, 'Exit' became Bono facing his own personal darkness by stepping into the mind of a killer as an allegory about the devastating effects of life on the fringes of American society. Adam expanded on this theme, saying he also saw the song as a critique of America's tarnished record on international relations. The authors that Bono was reading were having a direct influence on his growth as a songwriter, with him saying, 'The new American writers, especially the Southern ones, tend to write in a very direct way.'

Sadly, the song would carry new meaning

as life tragically imitated art. In 1989, Robert John Bardo was convicted of the murder of actor Rebecca Schaeffer, saying he was inspired by the lyrics of 'Exit'. As the song was played in court, Bardo was seen bobbing his head and lip-synching the lyrics. U2 performed 'Exit' throughout The Joshua Tree Tour, but the lyrics and the aftermath of Bardo's trial were taking its toll. The Edge said, 'Sometimes Bono would come offstage in the break and would not have left character. The darkness would still be there with him. Sometimes it was hard for him to shake it off and get into playing the next songs. That darkness has a certain kind of adrenaline.'

Despite its bleakness, though, U2 found much to celebrate about American culture – specially its music which introduced them to a much larger world. Growing up in Ireland in the 1970s, there were few opportunities to hear new music because, as the Edge told *CMJ*, there was only one national station that played rock music. Before touring there, U2 had believed American radio was too commercial and inaccessible to them because they did not sound like other rock bands. It was with the support of college radio stations, which had become a bastion for progressive music, that U2 were able to stake a foothold with American listeners. 'The college radio stations were crucial to U2 becoming known in the American radio world,' the Edge said.

U2 were also discovering American culture through public radio. Before recording *The Joshua Tree*, U2 had felt musically stifled, but their discovery of American blues and roots music on public radio reignited their creativity. In *U2 by U2*, the Edge remembers being disinterested in exploring American roots music as U2's inspiration, saying he had initially dismissed it because he thought it would be like the white-appropriated blues he heard on Irish radio. It was touring for *The Unforgettable Fire*, hearing artists like Robert Johnson and Howlin' Wolf on public radio, which made him reconsider tapping into America's musical heritage for their next album.

'Trip Through Your Wires', a rough and

Rebecca Schaeffer, 1987.

tumble blues jam, was one of the first songs that came together early in the album sessions. Though U2 were encouraged to work out song parts before recording, there was still much spontaneity in the studio. On the song, Bono said, 'We kind of made it up at the moment and I just blew into the harp. The thing about Dan Lanois and Brian Eno in the studio is that they're very supportive of ideas.' Just as it was the first song developed for *The Joshua Tree*, it was also the first U2 publicly premiered to show off their new-found American influence. In outfits that *Hot Press* editor Niall Stokes described as them looking like 'extras from some B-movie remake of *Easy Rider*', U2 performed 'Trip Through Your Wires' on RTÉ, coupled with an awkward blues song called 'Womanfish' they never recorded.

This influence of American roots is heard throughout the album. 'Running to Stand Still', a song about an Irish couple grappling with heroin addiction as a commentary on Dublin's urbanization, came together quickly in the studio. While the Edge tinkered with some piano chords, Lanois started playing guitar alongside him while the rest of the band followed. The Edge's slide acoustic guitar opening, added as one of the few overdubs, elevated the American roots aesthetic.

While U2 were becoming more connected with American musical traditions, they also found they could look to their own cultural traditions for inspiration as well. When Bob Dylan came to Slane Castle to wrap up his 1984 European tour, Bono went to interview him for *Hot Press*. During the interview, Bono was also introduced to Van Morrison, and the three discussed Irish folk music traditions and songwriting. Bono told the two veteran songsmiths that U2 had no musical tradition, insisting that they carved their own space outside the traditional Irish music scene that surrounded them growing up. Dylan urged Bono to explore his heritage's musical history further. The implication was that Ireland's musical lineage could help open U2's songs, providing language and structure to build more cohesive ideas.

'Red Hill Mining Town' comes from U2 bridging American traditional music and that of their homeland. Inspired by the 1984–85 National Union of Mineworkers' strike that followed British Prime Minister Margaret Thatcher's decision to shutter unprofitable mines, 'Red Hill Mining Town' tells the story of a miner struggling to keep his marriage together amidst the hardship of the strike. Drawing inspiration from labour rights songs by Peggy Seeger and Bruce Springsteen, Bono became interested in telling the story of the families affected by the strike rather than the politics surrounding it, but struggled bringing it to the band.

Larry, in *U2 by U2*, described 'Red Hill Mining Town' as one of U2's lost songs for being unfinished lyrically and overproduced musically, saying further that the band was unsure of how to capture Bono's idea. This revealed their growing pains as a band. Though the song was included on *The Joshua Tree*, it was originally slated to be a single but the idea was scrapped. A music video was even produced, directed by Neil Jordan, with the band sweaty and banging around a mine as canaries fly around them. It would take another 30 years before U2 felt like they had finished it, issuing a new mix in 2017 as a single for Record Store Day that turned up the brass horns that were buried in the original album mix. They also performed it live for the first time in celebration of *The Joshua Tree*'s 30th anniversary.

U2 put out 'I Still Haven't Found What I'm Looking For' as a single instead of 'Red Hill Mining Town'. The song's structure came from a drum pattern by Larry that turned into a jam session demo called 'The Weather Girls'. Lanois told *Hot Press*, 'We always look for those beats that would qualify as a signature for the song ... And we just didn't want to let go of that beat, it was so unique.' The Edge then composed a chord sequence on an acoustic guitar and layered it over the beat, creating a melody that showed the song's potential.

Eno and Lanois were both fans of gospel music and introduced Bono to groups such as the Swan Silvertones and The Staples Singers. For *Classic Albums*, Lanois said, 'I've always liked gospel music and I encouraged Bono to take it to that place ... It was a very non-U2 thing to do at the time, to go up the street of gospel. I think it opened a door for them, to experiment with that territory.'

While Bono was vocalizing a melody for the song in the studio, the Edge handed him

a paper with a phrase he thought made for an interesting song title. Hearing Bono find the melody while singing that phrase, U2 realised they had found the song they were looking for. Honouring Black gospel tradition, with its emphasis on strong vocal harmonies and themes of spirituality, 'I Still Haven't Found What I'm Looking For' became U2's contribution to the music that was inspiring them. With lyrics centred on spiritual yearning, U2's take on gospel tradition reflected their deepening appreciation of American culture. The song earned U2 critical acclaim upon its release, hitting number one on the US *Billboard* Hot 100 thanks to a music video of them performing around Fremont Street in Las Vegas, and has become one of their most beloved hits and concert staples.

Their journey through the culture of the American heartland revealed more than just the country's complexities – it also exposed the personal struggles within U2. As U2 gained worldwide popularity, Bono became tormented by how much a rock-star lifestyle could affect his marriage. In *U2 by U2*, Bono said he struggled to find a balance between being an artist and a husband. Touring America was fulfilling his wanderlust, but he was also growing concerned about whether a family would prevent him from achieving his musical aspirations. Bono channelled this internal conflict into 'With Or Without You', *The Joshua Tree*'s first single and U2's first number one hit, saying, 'It's about how I feel in U2 at times – exposed.'

While several songs on *The Joshua Tree* came together through improvisational jamming, 'With Or Without You' had to be built in the studio. The early demos sounded too traditional and when the Edge could not improve it with a more ambient guitar part, Eno and Lanois gave up while Bono and Gavin Friday continued working on the song. The song was saved when Michael Brook, a Canadian musician the Edge had worked with for the soundtrack to the 1986 film *Captive*, sent him a guitar prototype he had built called the Infinite Guitar, which allowed notes to be sustained after being played. While Bono and Friday were in the control room listening to the backing track, they heard the Edge's sustained effects and were impressed with how they

Above: Croke Park, Dublin, 1987. Opposite: Bob Dylan performs with Bono, California, 1987.

sounded together. The sustained effect that is the distinguishing hallmark of 'With Or Without You' was recorded in two takes and sequenced into the final mix.

However, another track proved more difficult to complete. 'Where the Streets Have No Name', with lyrics written by Bono during his humanitarian trip to Ethiopia, came from a four-track demo the Edge worked on in his home before U2 returned to the studio to finish the album. In *U2 by U2*, the Edge recalled that as the sessions neared their end, he realized that the album lacked songs that could resonate with concert audiences, so he set out to make the ultimate live U2 song. The rest of the band struggled to record the song's time and signature changes, with Adam saying it was like trying to understand a foreign language. Lanois called it a 'science project song' and, like a professor, demonstrated the chord changes on a schoolhouse blackboard to the band.

Eno claimed nearly half of the recording sessions for *The Joshua Tree* were spent on that one song. Convinced U2 were never going to finish it, Eno attempted to erase the tapes through a staged accident but was stopped by engineer Pat McCarthy at the last moment. The final version ultimately came together after Steve Lillywhite mixed it using different takes.

With its wall of sound production and guitar arpeggio, the Edge achieved his mission of making 'Where the Streets Have No Name' U2's ultimate live song. With over 950 live performances, it has become one of U2's most popular songs. 'We can be in the middle of the worst gig in our lives, but when we go into that song, everything changes,' said Bono. 'The audience is on its feet, singing along with every word. It's like God suddenly walks through the room.' The song's music video played on heavy rotation on MTV, featuring U2 performing live on the rooftop of a Los Angeles liquor store in front of a huge crowd until they were shut down by police, a nod to The Beatles' final concert on the roof of Abbey Road Studios.

While much of *The Joshua Tree* is centred on U2's feelings about America, it is a deeply personal album in another way. 'One Tree Hill' is a tribute to the band's friend Greg Carroll, to

whom *The Joshua Tree* is dedicated. Carroll was a Māori man Bono had met in his hotel bar during a sleepless night in Auckland at the start of their 1984 tour across Australia and New Zealand. Bono's friendship with Carroll formed quickly after Carroll took him to see the city skyline from Maungakiekie, also known as One Tree Hill, a volcanic mound of great spiritual importance to the Māori people. It was a significant moment in Bono's life, saying in *U2 by U2* that it stays with him because of the sense of freedom he felt.

Because of his experience in the New Zealand music scene, working with local bands like Straight Flash and The New Entrants, Carroll was hired as part of U2's stage crew for the remainder of the tour. Carroll impressed the band so much that they brought him to Dublin to be their personal assistant. In Dublin, Carroll's friendship with the band deepened to the point where Carroll was considered as family, with Bono describing him in Rolling Stone as 'like a brother'.

Unfortunately, tragedy struck. On a rainy night in Dublin on 3 July 1986, Bono asked Carroll to take his motorbike home for him, not knowing it would be the last time they would see each other. When a car cut him off, Carroll swerved away, but the slick road conditions prevented him from coming to a safe stop and he fatally crashed into another car. Bono went back to New Zealand to bury his friend, in accordance with Māori tradition, and performed Bob Dylan's 'Knockin' on Heaven's Door' and The Beatles' 'Let It Be' in his honour.

Bono recorded the vocals for 'One Tree Hill' in a single take because the grief was overwhelming. 'It brought gravitas to the recording of *The Joshua Tree*,' said Bono in *U2 by U2*. 'We had to fill the hole in our heart with something very, very large indeed. We loved him so much.'

The Joshua Tree was released on 9 March 1987, receiving universal critical acclaim with many reviews calling it U2's best album yet. The album received four nominations

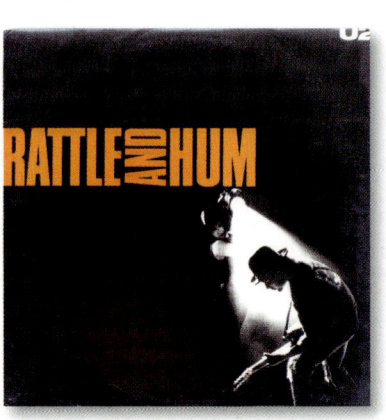

at the 1988 Grammys and won the award for Album of the Year. It was also a commercial juggernaut, topping charts in multiple countries, and has since become one of the world's bestselling albums ever with more than 25 million copies sold. A month after its release, U2 made the cover of *Time* as 'rock's hottest ticket'.

The Joshua Tree has also gained a reputation as one of the greatest and most influential albums of the last 40 years, achieving a legacy still felt today and proving that popular music can address social and political issues. In 2014, *The Joshua Tree* earned two major distinctions: being inducted into the Grammy Hall of Fame as well as the United States Library of Congress's National Recording Registry for its cultural importance.

With the success of *The Joshua Tree*, U2's audiences grew bigger. Performing 109 shows across the United States and Europe from April through December 1987, The Joshua Tree Tour saw U2 performing in larger venues, including stadiums, in order to meet demand. This was the first tour to stage rock music at such a scale. With its minimalist stage production, The Joshua Tree Tour became another outlet for U2 to unite music and politics. One example is before the tour's opening at Arizona State University's Activity Center on 2 April 1987, where U2 announced they had donated to a fund calling for the impeachment of Governor Evan Mecham over his vote against making Martin Luther King, Jr Day a holiday. Mr King, Jr was a figure U2 admired and who had influenced their music on *The Unforgettable Fire* and *The Joshua Tree*.

The Joshua Tree Tour also became the centrepiece of U2's second film. Directed by Phil Joanou and released theatrically by Paramount Pictures on 27 October 1988, with a title taken from a line in 'Bullet the Blue Sky', *Rattle and Hum* offered an immersive look at U2's travels across America as they explored the soul of its heartland. Including live performances from the tour as well as behind the scenes rehearsal footage and interviews with U2, Larry referred to *Rattle*

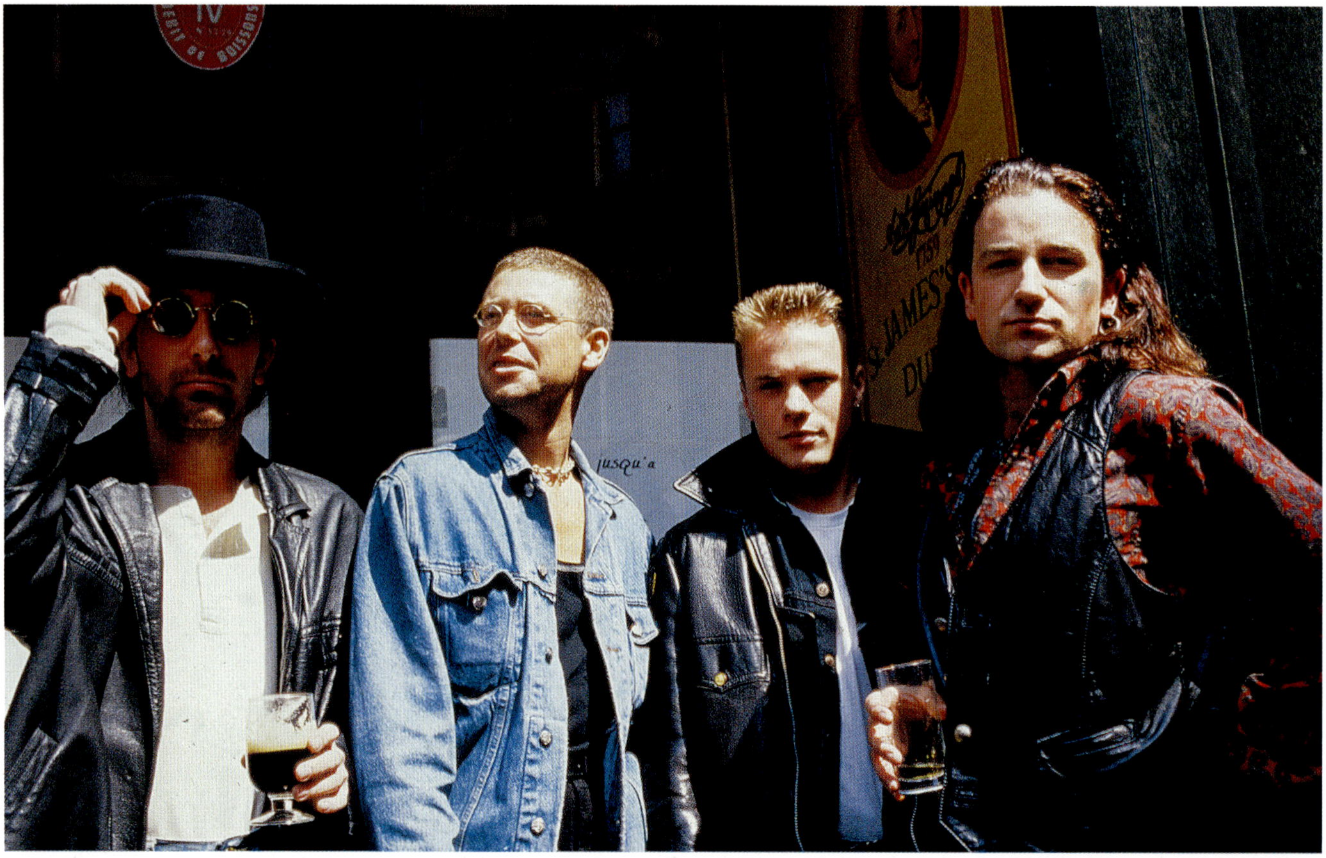
jusqu'a

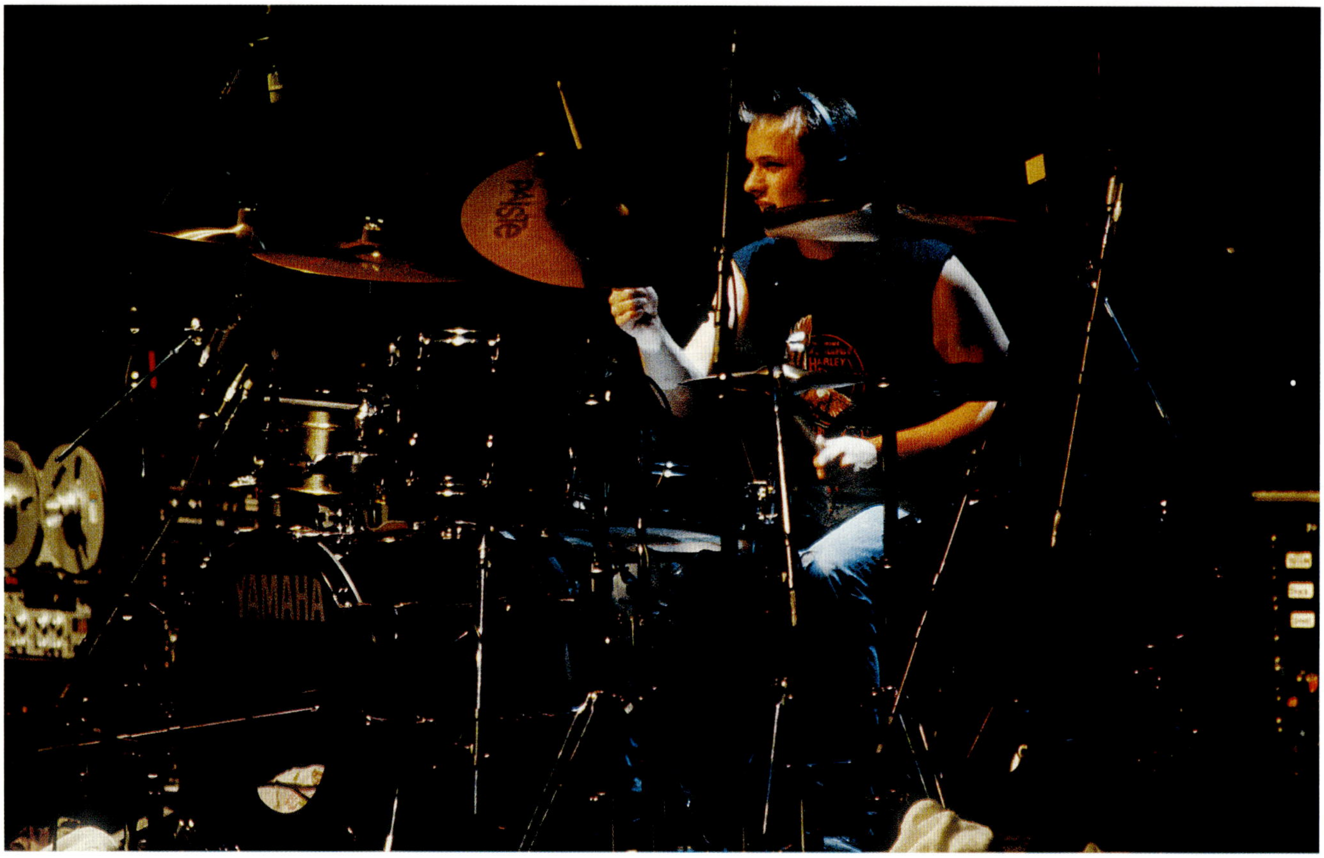
Paiste
YAMAHA

and Hum as a 'musical journey'.

Rattle and Hum notably captures the excitement of U2's concerts as one of rock's best live acts, with one of the film's highlights being their performance of 'Where the Streets Have No Name' at Sun Devil Stadium in Tempe, Arizona. During the song's synthesizer opening, the band walk out with their figures cast as silhouettes against the deep-red stage background as flashing lights set off when the music kicks in. Through sustained close-ups of the band's backlit figures, the cinematography reveals details of U2's performance that get lost in the grand scope of the stadium.

The film also captures an incredible moment in the band's history, showcasing the enduring relevance of their music. During the performance of 'Sunday Bloody Sunday' filmed in Denver, Bono quiets the band as he delivers an impassioned monologue condemning the Remembrance Day bombing committed by the Irish Republican Army in the Northern Ireland town of Enniskillen earlier that day and which killed 11 people, saying, 'I've had enough of Irish Americans who haven't been back to their country in 20 or 30 years come up to me and talk about the resistance, the revolution back home. And the glory of the revolution, and the glory of dying for the revolution. Fuck the revolution! They don't talk about the glory of killing for the revolution.' It is a starkly powerful moment with U2 refusing to play it safe as one of the biggest bands in the world. 'There are some people who say you shouldn't mix politics and music . . .', Adam says in the film. 'Well, I think that's kinda bullshit.'

The album companion, released on 10 October 1988, complements the beauty and bombast of the film. *Rattle and Hum* contains numerous tributes, opening with a live rendition of The Beatles' 'Helter Skelter' with Bono introducing it by saying, 'This is a song Charles Manson stole from The Beatles. We're stealing it back.' On their live version of 'All Along the Watchtower', U2 infuses Dylan's classic song with political urgency, with Bono adding to the original lyrics: 'All I got is a red guitar, three chords and the truth. All I got is a red guitar, the rest is up to you.' It is a delivery where U2 acknowledges their platform as politically engaged artists, but it is up to the people to use their power to take action.

The album also contains live renditions of earlier songs, including 'Pride (In the Name of Love)', 'Bullet the Blue Sky', and 'Silver and Gold'. Though, the defining live track from the album is the rendition of 'I Still Haven't Found What I'm Looking For', passionately performed with the gospel choir the New Voices of Freedom based out of Harlem. While the film only shows their rehearsal footage in church, both that and the live version recorded at Madison Square Garden are strikingly moving performances.

Rattle and Hum also includes several original songs that reveal America's continued influence on U2. 'Desire', with its Bo Diddley-inspired rhythm, blends fiery passion with critique of America's capitalist fundamentalist preachers. On 'Angel of Harlem', a song Bono wrote with Billie Holiday on his mind, the Memphis Horns takes U2's praise of New York's rich musical heritage and adds to it a joyous soulful sound.

Political and social messaging can also be heard throughout the original songs on *Rattle and Hum*. On 'God Part II', a spiritual successor to John Lennon's song 'God', Bono defends the legacy of his musical hero while also questioning whether rock music can really change the world. A song written and performed by the Edge, 'Van Diemen's Land' conveys the suffering and indignity that immigrants continue to endure. Originally written while recording *The Joshua Tree*, 'Heartland' stands out as U2's ode to a country that Bono says, 'both fascinates and frightens me'.

'All I Want Is You', the album's closer, remains one of U2's greatest love songs. 'It became a meditation on commitment and what that means,' said Bono. As the fourth single off *Rattle and Hum*, the song did not chart as well as the others. However, it would gain a resurgence in popularity several years later when it was included on the soundtrack for the 1994 film *Reality Bites*, resulting in a rerelease that charted higher than it did originally.

Rattle and Hum also includes several collaborations. Bob Dylan co-wrote the lyrics to 'Love Rescue Me' with Bono and plays the Hammond organ on 'Hawkmoon 269'. On 'When Love Comes to Town', U2 is joined by blues guitar legend B.B. King, a coupling that came about after Bono shoved a note with the lyrics under King's hotel room door. Allegedly,

Opposite top: Paris, 1987.
Opposite bottom: Larry Mullen Jr, Belgium, 1987.

King responded by asking Bono how old he was because he felt the lyrics were too heavy to be written by such a young man. They recorded the song at Sun Studios, a site of much importance to U2 since Elvis Presley had recorded there. 'You go into the Sun room, and it's a modest room,' Adam recalled, '… and you try to get back that feeling of making rock 'n' roll without having huge banks of Marshalls and whatever. Just strip it back and play the simplest thing you can.'

However, despite the success of *The Joshua Tree* and its ensuing tour, U2 were unable to earn the acclaim their first film, *Under a Blood Red Sky*, had achieved. Though it became the highest-grossing documentary at the time of its release, the film was much maligned by the press. As U2 had only achieved their success recently, critics felt tributes were misguided attempts to compare the band to iconic artists. '*Rattle and Hum* was conceived as a scrapbook, a memento of that time spent in America on The Joshua Tree Tour', said the Edge in *Revolver*. 'It changed when the movie, which was initially conceived of as a low-budget film, suddenly became a big Hollywood affair. That put a different emphasis on the album, which suffered from the huge promotion and publicity, and people reacted against it.'

U2 felt dragged down by their bad reviews and critics accusing them of megalomania. They learned a hard lesson that Americans were already aware of their own roots music which U2 had only recently discovered and then reintroduced back to American audiences from a foreign lens. U2 had creative control over the film's final edit and how they wanted to be seen, but the awe they sought to convey to audiences was instead seen as rock stars being self-important. It was a shock for U2 so soon after their recent success. 'You start to believe what people are saying about you,' said Bono in the documentary *From the Sky Down*.

With their creative impulses running on empty, U2's fascination with American roots music was turning them into the kind of overblown rock band they had always wanted to avoid becoming. 'This didn't become us,' said Bono in *From the Sky Down*. 'This was the enemy. Had we become the enemy?'

Following the release of *Rattle and Hum*, U2 embarked on the Lovetown Tour from September 1989 through January 1990, taking *The Joshua Tree* outside America to New Zealand, Australia and a few cities across Europe. While *The Joshua Tree* was a global success, U2 were coming to the end of their existential journey through the American mythos. They sensed they had overstayed their welcome and their minds had been elsewhere even before the Lovetown Tour ended. During U2's concert in Dublin on 30 December 1989, Bono addressed the audience saying, 'This is just the end of something for U2. And that's why we're playing these concerts – and we're throwing a party for ourselves and you. It's no big deal, it's just – we have to go away and … and dream it all up again.'

When U2 sought to redefine their sound, it was the beginning of a new journey for the band. Their restlessness had served them well back then, making sure they did not stay in one place too long. However, that feeling was returning and a choice needed to be made. U2 were a world away from where they were when they put out their first album at the start of a decade that was now ending, but a new one was dawning with untold possibilities over the horizon. As U2 stepped out of the silver-sanded monochromatic desert of the 1980s and into the Technicolor metropolis of the 1990s, they would don new masks to become even better than the real thing.

Bono, 1989.

3

One

The critical backlash U2 received at the close of the 1980s left them feeling rattled and humdrum. It was an alienating experience for them, with Bono

saying in *From the Sky Down* that Ireland saw U2 as the enemy for abandoning their post-punk roots and returning home as an obnoxious American showband. Under the pressure of figuring out what was next, a rift was forming within the band.

With the arrival of the 1990s, several music scenes defined the European cultural landscape. When the fall of the Berlin Wall reunified Germany, underground electronic music emerged from the rubble. German techno, which was influenced by electric pioneers like Kraftwerk and Tangerine Dream, and industrial noise rock, with its avant-garde roots in Can and Neu!, became thriving subcultures that found refuge turning abandoned buildings, often factory relics or concrete ruins from World War II, into makeshift nightclubs where the environment both reflected and drove the music. 'Something about that new decade, the '90s, something about the fall of the Berlin Wall, a new Europe emerging; that's what we were focusing on,' said the Edge in *From the Sky Down*.

The Edge had become fascinated with electronic and industrial music, listening to bands like KMFDM, Einstürzende Neubauten and The Young Gods. The machine music that came from electronic and industrial was, said the Edge, about 'taking the humanity out of things to a degree so that the humanity that you put in there means more.' These artists shared similar roots with U2 as Kraftwerk also influenced them, a common musical ancestry Bono refers to in *From the Sky Down* as 'soul music from Europe'.

Outside Germany, U2 also had their eyes on the Madchester scene coming out of England. Pioneered by groups like Happy Mondays and The Stone Roses, this convergence of alternative indie music with acid house and retro pop both perplexed and interested U2. In *U2 by U2*, Adam said they did not connect with the scene's musical nostalgia but appreciated its emphasis on rhythm and percussion loops. With the arrival of a new Europe for the 1990s, U2 were thrilled to observe rock 'n' roll and club culture colliding to form something original and innovative.

Though unsure of what their next album would sound like, U2 found opportunities to work

Previous page: Portrait
shot, 1990.
Opposite: Bono, 1990.

on new material that hinted at their potential creative trajectory. For *Red Hot + Blue* – a compilation album featuring contemporary artists reimagining Cole Porter songs to raise money for the AIDS activist group ACT UP – U2 recorded an electronic version of 'Night and Day' from the 1932 musical *Gay Divorce* that updated it by blending industrial and hip-hop elements. Bono and the Edge also recorded 'Alex Descends into Hell for a Bottle of Milk/Korova 1', an industrial-influenced score composed for a theatrical adaptation of Anthony Burgess's 1962 dystopian novel *A Clockwork Orange*. U2 also spent time recording demos at Dublin's STS studios, but were not making much progress. These were glimpses of U2 trying to find themselves.

Morale had dropped and the band were not speaking with each other much. In *From the Sky Down*, Larry recalls Bono and the Edge taking off to develop new songs and not really hearing from them until just before they started recording. Larry spent this downtime taking drum lessons while Adam was experiencing personal issues. 'There was a little bit of abandonment,' said Adam.

In desperate need of a distraction from their disappointment, U2 decided to leave Dublin and escape to Berlin, hoping to reinvigorate their sound, bringing along Brian Eno and Daniel Lanois to help them find their footing. U2 chose to record their new album at Hansa Studios, a Weimar Republic-era former cabaret and chamber music hall, following in the footsteps of their music heroes David Bowie and Iggy Pop who recorded several classic albums there such as *Low*, *'Heroes'* and *The Idiot*. Eno introduced U2 to Hansa since he was already familiar with the space having previously worked with Bowie there and felt they could develop a sophisticated groove and rhythm 'somewhere where there was a culture collision going on' and where they could 'let the thing kind of go out of control'.

U2's vision for their new album was to tap into the club culture and infuse it with rhythmic groove rock without sounding clichéd. 'We were running away from Lovetown and *Rattle and Hum* as fast as we could,' said the Edge. Instead of returning to the slick retro stylings of the Jimmy Iovine-produced *Rattle and Hum*, U2 turned again to Eno's Oblique Strategies to help guide

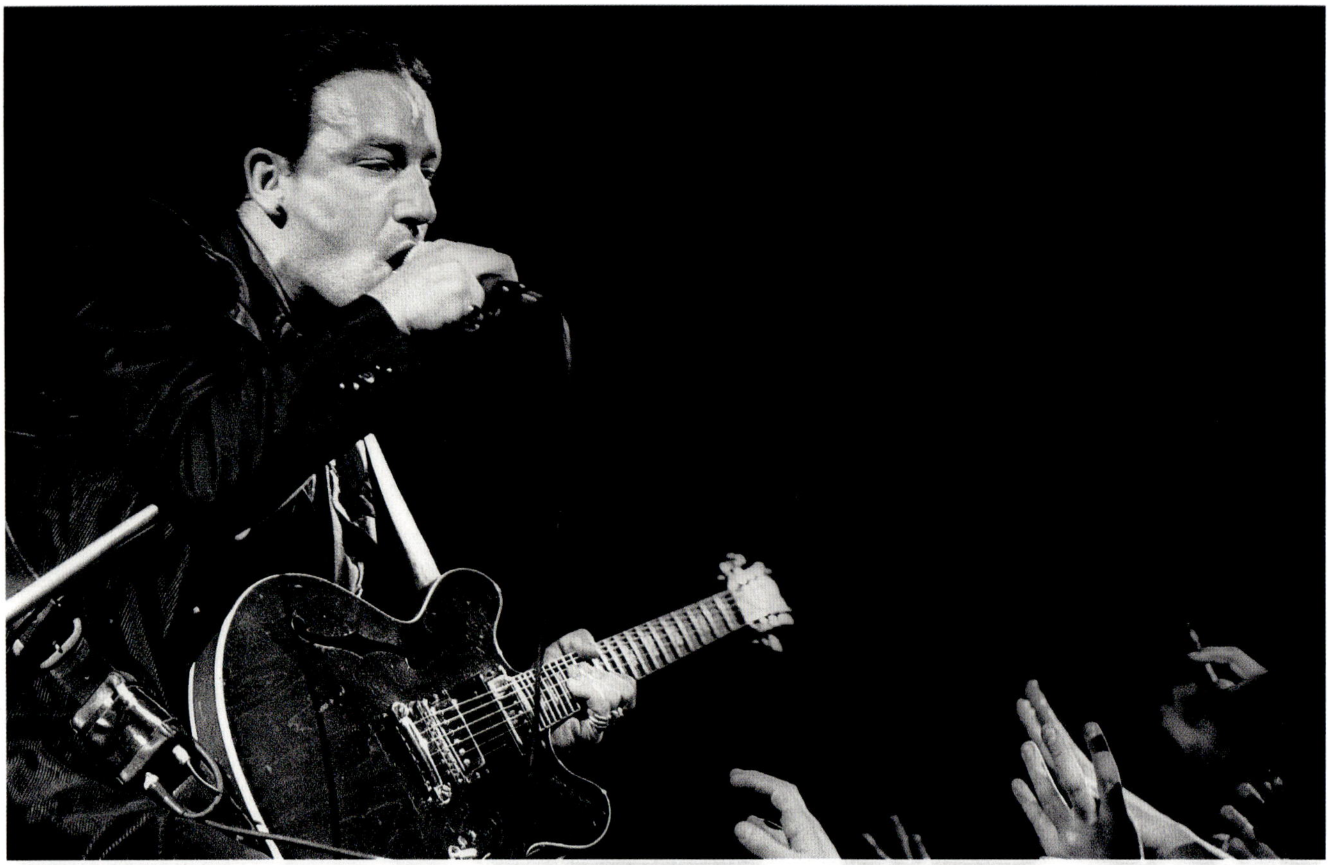

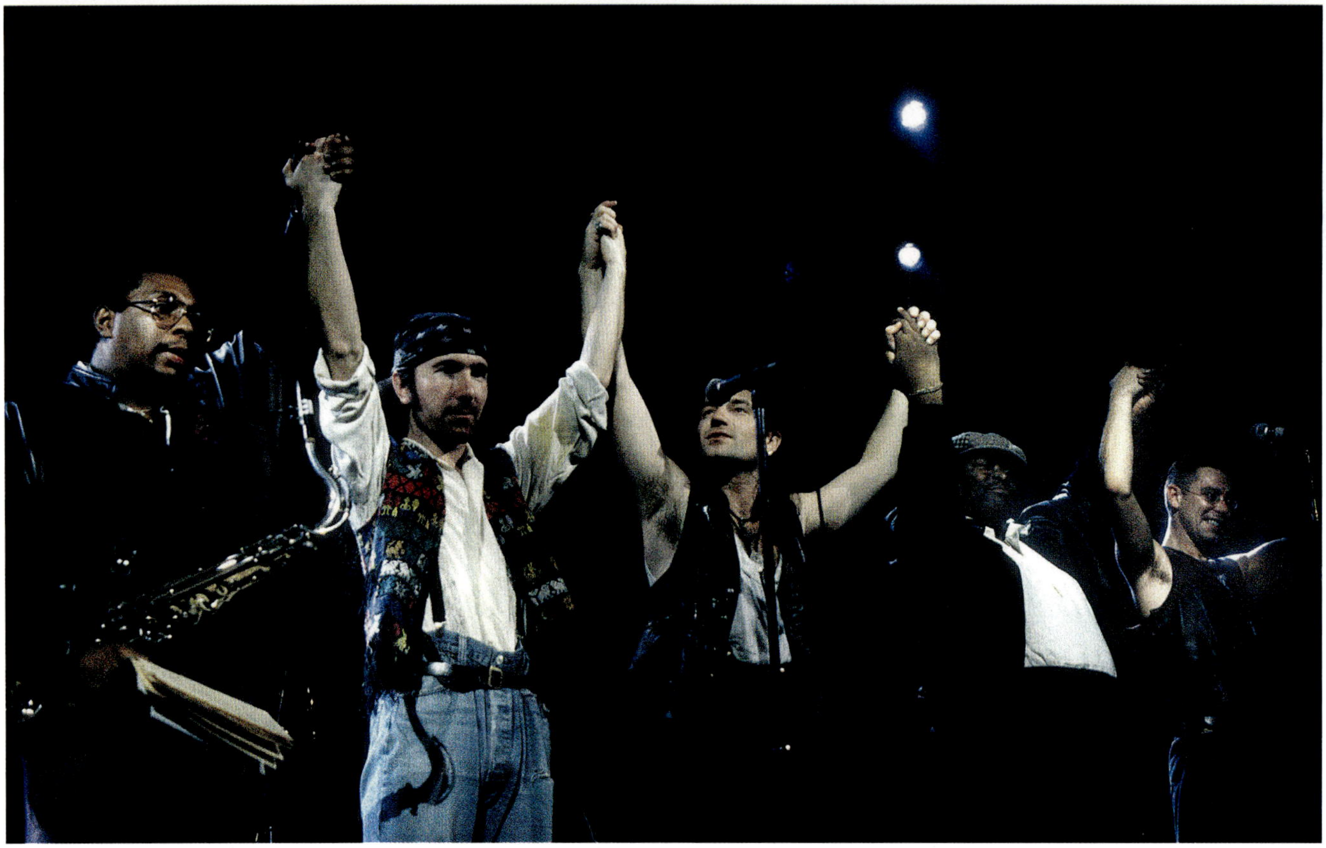

them, using philosophical problem-solving to help them navigate their new sound. As before, Lanois was there to balance out Eno's ambience with harder rock that brought out the recent techno and industrial influences on U2.

Unfortunately, the new Europe's shine was fading when U2 started recording at Hansa, with the gloomy drabness of Berlin in winter matching the dismal mood brewing inside. A malaise had settled once the reunification fervour quietened down.

U2 had recorded demos at STS Studios in Dublin before going to Berlin, some of which would evolve and find their way on to the album, but the magic was missing in Hansa. 'Even before we went [to Berlin], there was a sense that something was not quite right,' said Larry. 'And when we got there, we were on completely different pages.'

At Hansa, U2 approached the sessions the same way they had done with earlier albums, which was to find the spirit of the song through improvisation. Adam recalled the goal 'was to look for the magic moment when we play together'. Bono and the Edge wanted U2 to try new things, but they had trouble communicating ideas to the others, which had created division even before U2 left for Berlin. They often did not include Adam and Larry in the songwriting process, a creative shift that had begun while recording *The Joshua Tree*, which led to miscommunication on what to do for the new album. Larry recalls not understanding back then that Bono and the Edge were trying to bring in electronic influences, saying further that he became resistant to their ideas because of that. Larry at the time was being driven more by the classic rock he discovered, like Cream and Jimi Hendrix, and questioned why the band needed to sound like they were no longer U2. Larry was also frustrated by the modern technology being used in the studio, the drum machine making him feel like he was no longer contributing to the music because the drums had taken a back seat to Bono and the Edge exploring club music.

The band jammed for hours, trying out new rhythms and ideas. However, they did not like the material and could not agree on what to do next, resulting in a lot of arguments during the sessions. Bono called the atmosphere in Hansa a 'long, cold existence'. Bono and

Previous spread top left: Bono, Netherlands, 1990.; bottom left: U2 perform on stage with BB King on the LoveTown Tour, Netherlands,1990.; Previous spread right: Adam Clayton and Bono during the Zoo TV Tour at Wembley Stadium, London, 1993.
Opposite: Zoo TV Tour in London, 1993.

Lanois had even almost fought each other during one session. In another, Adam became so frustrated with Bono's criticism that he handed his bass guitar to Bono and said, 'You tell me what to play and I'll play it. You want to play it yourself? Go ahead.'

Cracks were forming in their foundation of friendship. They were no longer having fun like the boys they were when they started out, now drifting apart as too-serious men. Unable to find a common language in Hansa, everyone in U2 retreated to their own corner. Bono said it was a situation with 'each man for himself, which is a betrayal of the concept of a band'.

However, it was during their darkest moment that U2's vulnerability ignited a spark that would burn brightly enough to become one of their greatest artistic achievements. Mark Ellis – the album's engineer also known as Flood – on the sessions said, 'It's fraught with danger because you can fail at any moment but that's the whole beauty of it; if you're prepared to remove the safety net and if you're prepared to really expose yourselves, because your pursuit is after the magic moments. Those moments of "Wow! I would never have imagined."' It was during one such magic moment that the walls came tumbling down.

U2 were rehearsing an early session song they referred to as 'Sick Puppy', a jam experimenting with different chord progressions for the bridge. On the electric guitar, the Edge played a new melody for the first bridge and then later played a second new bridge. The energy in the room immediately changed following the second bridge. Lanois then suggested that the Edge play the bridges sequentially, with him also performing both on an acoustic guitar.

The band were eager to follow this new idea, stopping their rehearsal of 'Sick Puppy' and instead working to form a whole new song around this bridge. Telling the Edge to give him 'an acoustic guitar at the speed of light', Bono experimented with various vocal melodies, a part of his songwriting process where he scat sings in a faux language style he calls Bongolese. Adam recalled Bono calling out chords and moving chords around to find 'where the fertile ground is for him melodically'.

It soon become clear that something powerfully moving was coming together. The

Edge recalled that this song forming became a gift that arrived in the studio and steadied everyone's nerves. It was a pivotal moment in what had been a difficult journey.

This moment of inspiration that brought U2 back together became 'One'. A song about relationships, both within U2 and outside of them, 'One' represents a much bigger ideal than unity. When it looked like U2 were no longer happy playing together, Bono said that first performance of 'One' became the true meaning of the song. 'We are one, but we're not the same,' said Bono of the song in *U2 by U2*. 'It's not saying we even want to get along, but that we have to get along together in this world if it is to survive. It's a reminder that we have no choice.' U2 could now stand together to finish what they started.

U2 returned to Dublin in December 1990 and finished the album in February 1991, choosing to record in a seaside mansion called Elsinore for its elusiveness and sonic qualities. Not feeling like strangers in a strange land anymore, the relaxed mood allowed the sessions to become much less tense and more productive.

U2 had discovered a lot during their musical exploration resulting in them having recorded an abundance of material. Additional engineers were brought in to sort through everything, coming up with solutions like holding secondary sessions at the Edge's home studio and customizing equipment to record overdubs and alternative takes using 48 makeshift audio tracks instead of the standard 24. The band were rushing to finish the album before their September deadline, working so close to the last minute that they did not even finalize the track listing until the day before the master tapes were due.

Two months later, on 18 November 1991, U2 released *Achtung Baby* which reintroduced them to the world. Combining alternative rock with industrial and electronic dance music, *Achtung Baby* presented a darker and more deeply personal U2. Stripping themselves of the anthemic rock style that defined their 1980s sound, U2 entirely reinvented their image and music for a new age and audience.

Keeping a low profile to avoid the crosshairs of the press, U2 did not issue advanced copies of the album to reviewers and instead preferred to have word spread through their fans. *Achtung Baby* earned wide critical and commercial acclaim, topping the charts in multiple countries as U2's third number one album and allowing them to reassert their position as one of the biggest bands in the world.

One of the biggest changes to U2's sound came from the Edge's guitar playing. Instead of a minimalist approach accompanied by heavy delays, the Edge created a harsher and more metallic texture with his guitar to create heavy distortion and feedback effects. On 'Zoo Station', the album's opener, the guitar effect at the beginning was intended to make the listener think they bought the wrong album. On 'Even Better Than the Real Thing', the riff during the chorus shows off U2's playfulness by featuring the influence of dance music on the album, spawning several remixes that heightened the song's appeal in the clubs.

As much as the Edge's guitar sound had progressed, it is really complemented by both Larry and Adam's contributions which truly capture U2's creative progress on *Achtung Baby*. Larry becomes more dynamic with his drumming style, transitioning between hip-hop, electronic and industrial beats to create a diverse rhythmic flow for the album. Adam's bass also brings out the central groove that reveals the album's danceability.

The elements Larry and Adam brought were integral during the early sessions. 'Mysterious Ways', which originated from the groove laid down by Adam and Larry during the 'Sick Puppy' jam, is one of U2's funkiest songs. Besides 'One', it was the only other song U2 completed at Hansa. 'Mysterious Ways' also adds vibrant sensuality to the album, featuring lyrics of a man crawling towards a woman as a supreme being. Morleigh Steinberg, an American choreographer who performs as a belly dancer in the music video, would later marry the

Previous spread: Fans at the Zoo TV Tour. Opposite: The Edge in Paris, 1993.

Edge, adding a personal connection to the song.

Thematically and lyrically, *Achtung Baby* is a more personal work than U2's earlier albums. Many songs throughout are intimate and introspective, often swirling sexuality and spirituality into narratives about relationships with lovers, God and when both seemingly become one. As the first song completed, 'One' sets the conceptual tone for *Achtung Baby*, but each song reveals a new layer for the listener. 'Mysterious Ways' and 'Even Better Than the Real Thing' add sex appeal to the album's nightlife side, but 'Tryin' to Throw Your Arms Around the World' is the morning after when you stumble back home into the arms of the one who waited.

The relationship theme combines with the divine for 'Until the End of the World'. Though originally conceived for the 1991 Wim Wenders science-fiction film *Until the End of the World*, Bono had been reading Irish author Brendan Kennelly's poem collection *The Book of Judas* which examines Judas Iscariot as an allegory for man's complexities and explores the hypothetical question of whether anyone can truly achieve grace. Inspired by some trouble in Bono and the Edge's own friendship, the lyrics of the song carry the spirit of Kennelly's book.

Other songs on *Achtung Baby* explore the hurt that can come from relationships. 'Ultraviolet (Light My Way)' takes Bono's restlessness and turns it into a crisis of faith, perhaps in terms of both his lover and his lord. 'So Cruel' is about the anguishing over the bitterness and betrayal one feels after being scorned while 'Who's Gonna Ride Your Wild Horses' conveys the longing that comes when a lover leaves.

Some songs from *Achtung Baby* feel so personal precisely because they came from real life. The Edge separated from his wife Aislinn O'Sullivan during the recording of *Achtung Baby* and, while his feelings are channelled throughout the album, this comes through most prominently on the closing two tracks. 'Acrobat' is about how confusion comes in different forms, often through cynicism and feelings of inadequacy. The centrepiece is the Edge's guitar solo which takes the industrial influence of Sonic Youth and My Bloody Valentine. Bono described 'Acrobat' as a 'song about being a hypocrite' expressed as

an acrobat bending so many ways to please someone, even at their own expense.

The closing track, 'Love Is Blindness', uses violent terroristic imagery to signify a failing relationship. Bono said in *U2 by U2* that the song conveys an emotional landmine that later blows a relationship apart when accidentally triggered. The impact of the Edge's marriage failing not only affected the recording of *Achtung Baby*, but also the extended U2 family. Bono said in *From the Sky Down*, 'We're a really tight community. This is not like somebody's, you know, girlfriend left. We've grown up with these people; this is our family, our community. This was really hard for us … It was like the first cracks on the beautiful porcelain jug with those beautiful flowers in it that was our music and our community, starting to go "crack".'

Closing out 'Love Is Blindness' and the album is a guitar solo that the Edge put all his pain and fury into. In Michka Assayas' book, Bono said, 'I was pushing him and pushing him and pushing him, and he played until the strings fell off. Actually, you'll hear strings snapping during the solo towards the end. He was, I think, in tears on the inside, and the outside was just raging.'

Bono's vocals on *Achtung Baby* also highlight the new U2. On previous albums, Bono's tenor vocals were grandiose powerful gestures. For *Achtung Baby*, Bono's vocals have a lower and more emotional timbre which he said allowed him to find a new vocal vocabulary. Using different octaves, 'The Fly' is one track where Bono's vocals truly shine. Bono performs in different registers, juxtaposing his deeper and higher tones, which creates thematic atmosphere in the song. Released as *Achtung Baby*'s first single, Bono described 'The Fly' as 'the sound of four men chopping down *The Joshua Tree*'.

'The Fly' as the first single also symbolized U2's new image and persona. Dutch photographer Anton Corbijn captured U2's musical journey during the 1980s with elegant black-and-white portraits, but critics felt they made U2 appear humourless and stone-faced. The excitement of the 1990s required a complete visual overhaul, focusing on bright colourful images to contrast their achromatic reputation. Corbijn photographed the band in the Canary Islands and Morocco, and in exotic situations, like mingling with carnival

Opposite top: Zoo TV Tour in New York. Opposite below: Ticket Stub for the Zoo TV Tour at Wembley Stadium, London, 1993.

crowds and dressing in drag. In Berlin, where the landscape was more subdued, Corbijn photographed U2 alongside artistically decorated Trabants, small East German cars that symbolized communism's economic stagnation and which became an icon for that period of U2's career. 'We started to embrace our world and the silliness of it; the contradictory nature of it. We stopped trying to be those earnest, po-faced men,' said Adam in *From the Sky Down*. 'It was a move into brighter life.'

'You have to reject one expression of the band first before you can get to the next expression,' said Bono, 'and in between you have nothing.'

The cover for *Achtung Baby*, designed by Steve Averill, captures the journey towards this next expression, featuring a grid of Corbijn's photos chosen for their expressiveness and ambiguity. The album title, calligraphed by Shaughn McGrath, is a German translation of 'attention baby' and comes from a line performed by Mel Brooks in 'To Be or Not to Be (The Hitler Rap)' for the soundtrack of his 1983 remake of the film *To Be or Not to Be*. Bono told *Rolling Stone* that the title is 'a con, in a way. We call it *Achtung Baby*, grinning up our sleeves in all the photography. But it's probably the heaviest record we've ever made … It tells you a lot about packaging, because the press would have killed us if we'd called it anything else.'

All the visual and musical qualities of the album combine to form Bono's alter ego, the Fly. Sporting a skintight leather outfit and black bug-eyed wrap-around sunglasses, the Fly is a caricature of an egomaniacal rock star that became a creative catharsis for Bono as a stage performer. Borrowing fashion elements from famous rock stars including Lou Reed's sunglasses, Jim Morrison's pants and Elvis Presley's jacket and haircut, Bono crafted the Fly as an assembled 'identikit rock star'.

While his namesake song and its accompanying music video introduced him to U2's fans, the Fly truly takes flight on Zoo TV. Their first tour after a nearly two-year public performance hiatus, and kicking off in the United States during February 1992, Zoo TV saw U2 taking their reinvention worldwide but in a much bigger way. While earlier tours had production design that was sparse and minimalistic, Zoo TV represented a 180-degree turn as a sensory overloading multimedia experience. The complex stage design included several dozen screens, flanked by hanging colourful Trabants retrofitted with spotlights, which displayed different video feeds including footage of the band performing, live satellite broadcasts and rapidly flashing text and visual graphics, all colliding to create a concert experience rooted in maximalist minimalism. According to the Edge in *Hot Press*, the technology allowed the band to become more spontaneous and flexible as stage performers since they could use stage elements to create a unique live experience.

During the concert opener 'Zoo Station', Bono would emerge onstage as the Fly with his silhouette appearing against the flashing video screens. The Edge told Zoo Radio that the concert opening represented 'four minutes of a television that's not tuned into any station, but giving you interference and shash and almost a TV picture'. Both on- and offstage, the Fly gave Bono a particular feeling of escape as he often stayed in character as a way to say things he could not otherwise say himself.

This character dynamic is just one highlight of the satirical concept behind Zoo TV. The tour's visuals, from the presentation to the images themselves, were used as performance art that took a funhouse mirror to mass media. By showing footage including news coverage of the Gulf War, game shows, soap operas, home shopping, sport matches and other programmes to create the effect of a pirate television station, U2 wanted to critique how desensitized the public had become to seeing all this content distilled as entertainment and competing for profit. The visuals provided a commentary on how the media made both the macabre and the mundane become one.

Bono also stepped into two other characters to enhance the media commentary for Zoo TV. Bono's criticism of American televangelists goes back to before *The Joshua Tree*, but he embodied an extreme version of one for Zoo TV. The Mirror Ball Man, a Southern preacher in a shiny silver lamé suit and cowboy hat, is Bono mocking the holy rolling snake oil salesmen who held cultural and political sway throughout the Reagan administration and now into the George H. W. Bush presidency.

Opposite: Bono as 'The Fly'.
Next spread: Bono as 'MacPhisto', 1993.

As the Mirror Ball Man, Bono would perform outrageous stunts like making prank phone calls to the White House and asking to be put in contact with the president. He would also do other eccentric things like throw fake dollar bills into the audience, call a phone sex number and he even once ordered ten thousand pizzas, of which 100 were actually delivered and handed out to the front-row audience. The Mirror Ball Man was a critique of prosperity gospel with Bono saying in *U2 by U2* that the character's fortune was proof that God did not make mistakes.

The Mirror Ball Man was later replaced by another egomaniacal character for the European legs of the tour. Dressed this time in a gold lamé suit with platform shoes, Bono donned white make-up and devil horns to become MacPhisto. A flamboyant ageing European rock star, MacPhisto represented a darker comedy not expressed through the Fly's hedonism. Bono as MacPhisto would pester political leaders over the phone as well as regale the audience with monologues about his power, influence and fame. MacPhisto would make claims to the audience such as that he gave Americans president Bill Clinton, got Europe to quit arguing by connecting them to cable television and that he brought capitalism to the former Soviet Union. Bono would refer to MacPhisto as 'the Fly when he's old, fat and playing Vegas'.

Not just all irony, U2's music was still a platform for political activism. In Manchester on 19 June 1992, Zoo TV became an environmental benefit concert. Organized by Greenpeace, U2 headlined the Stop Sellafield concert to protest at plans to expand a reactor at the Sellafield nuclear plant which had been dumping waste along the coast of Cumbria in northern England. Supported by a trio of politically engaged openers that included Kraftwerk, Public Enemy and Big Audio Dynamite II, U2 used the full technical might of Zoo TV to shift the tide of power and public opinion, flashing words like 'fallout', 'plutonium', 'mutant', 'radiation', 'sickness' and 'Chernobyl' on its massive video screens. The day after the show, U2 joined other protesters on boats delivering radioactive sand to the beach at Sellafield as a protest message to the plant and the media.

After finishing the North American 'Outside Broadcast' leg of Zoo TV in November 1992,

U2 took a six-month break before touring resumed. Instead of resting up, U2 wanted to harness their energy coming off the tour to write and record new music they could promote throughout the summer of 1993 during the *Zooropa* leg that would take them around Europe.

U2 were energized to build on the momentum of their musical reinvention. As Zoo TV progressed, the industrial and electronic dance elements of their music came to the fore. The idea was to create an EP showing their musical evolution that they could use to promote the tour, but time was limited. Fortunately, U2 had recorded their concert soundchecks throughout Zoo TV and, to get things started for the EP, they asked sound mixer Robbie Adams to use them to create loop samples. With Brian Eno and Flood returning to help produce, U2 began working on demo recordings using those soundcheck loops.

It became apparent early on that U2 had a lot of material to work with, but they had no vision for the music and were unsure of how long it would take to finish. The question then became whether U2 could release new music before going back on tour or if these sessions were drafts of something much bigger.

The Edge wanted U2 to stick with their original plan to record an EP, recalling in *U2 by U2* that they had enough musical ideas that fans would enjoy while also breathing new life into the tour. However, as the sessions continued and U2 recorded more material, there was growing interest in expanding the EP into a whole album. Encouraged by Bono, the Edge became convinced about the idea of recording an album after recognizing how this kind of challenge could push U2 out of their comfort zones as artists. 'We thought we could go into a decompression chamber and come out the other end normal,' Bono told *Spin* in 1993, 'but it turns out that your whole way of thinking, your whole body has been geared towards the madness of Zoo TV … so we decided to put the madness on a record.'

During March 1993, with only two months left before they continued their tour, U2 went back to recording using lessons they learned from making *Achtung Baby*. To maximize the time to achieve their ambitious album goal, U2 set up dual sessions at the Factory and Windmill Lane Studios which became

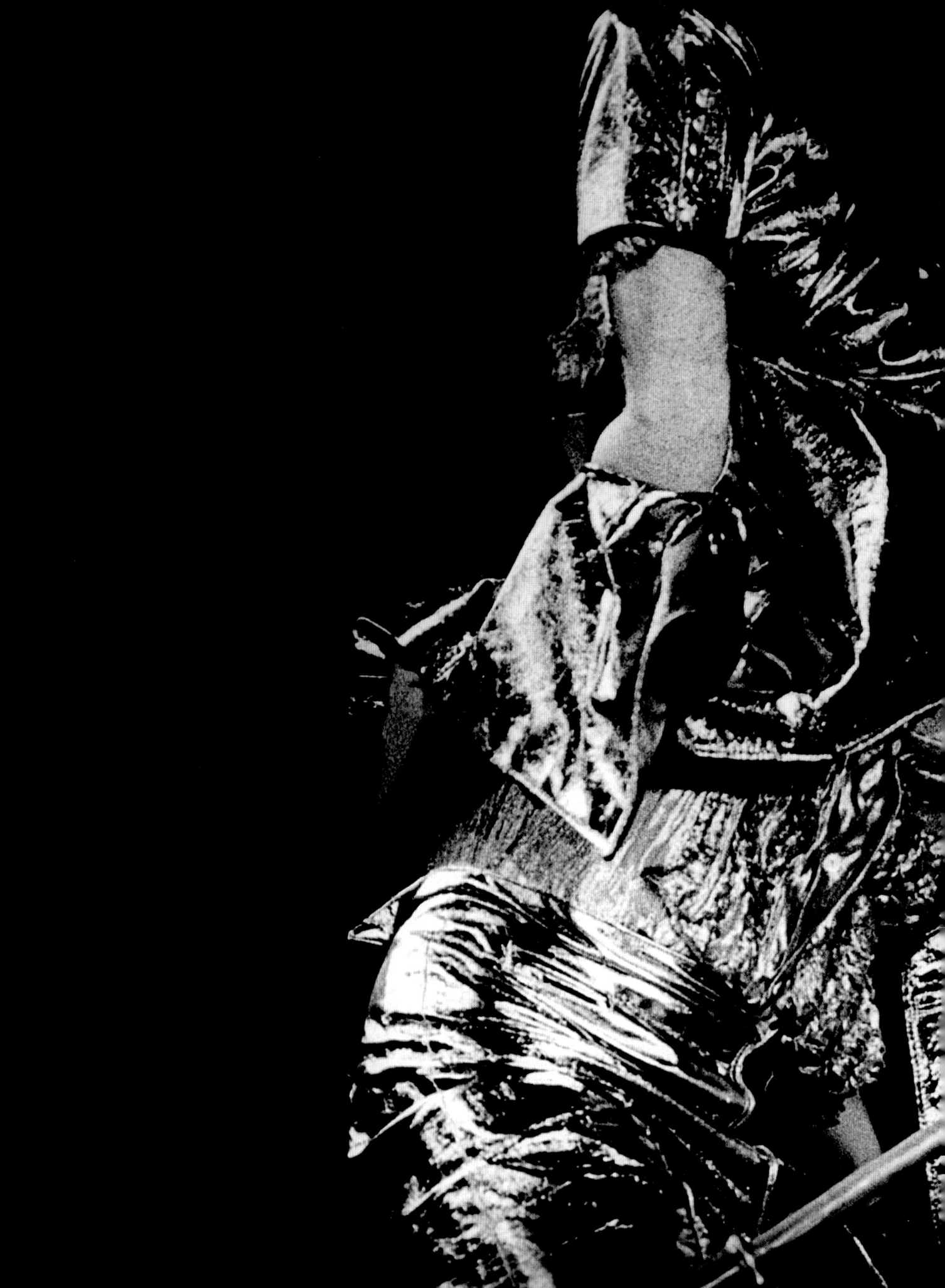

essential due to the amount of material that required different technical approaches. Unlike on *Achtung Baby*, guitar riffs became less of a priority, with U2 instead spending their time on loop samples Adams compiled which ultimately changed the aesthetic direction of the album. In a 1994 interview with *Sound on Sound*, Adams said, 'U2 don't use loops taken from other people's records so instead I made loops of Larry drumming. That worked quite well and several of the loops ended up on the record.'

As U2's recording dynamic was shifting, the Edge became more involved in studio production. Filling in the gap left by U2's other frequent collaborator, Daniel Lanois, who was busy touring his solo album, the Edge told *Rolling Stone*, 'I suppose I took on a level of responsibility that I hadn't on previous records. That meant sitting in with Bono on lyric writing sessions … down to completely demoing some pieces, establishing their original incarnations … and then, generally, just worrying more than everyone else.'

U2 worked diligently in the studio but were unable to complete recording before the tour, which also meant they could not rehearse live arrangements of the new songs. As the tour resumed, U2 flew back to Dublin on their days off to finish the album, expanding to three rooms in Windmill Lane to speed up the process. 'I'd be in the studio until three or four in the morning,' said the Edge, 'and then going home, getting up the next day and getting on a plane at lunchtime, going off doing a show, coming back at 1 a.m., staying up again till 4 a.m. [It] was pretty mind-numbing by the end.'

U2 released their spontaneous new album *Zooropa* on 5 July 1993, five months after they began recording and only two months into the tour leg. The Edge earned a producer credit for his contributions on the album as well as elevating the distortion and hip-hop beats of the loops to broaden U2's sound and aesthetic. Relying on the drum machine more, a device that had become a point of contention while recording *Achtung Baby*, the Edge used it as a tool to refine U2's creative

process. Larry said, 'Edge was still exploring dance and hip-hop culture, club mixes, all that kind of thing. He was experimenting and U2 were his guinea pigs.' While ideas for *Achtung Baby* evolved during Zoo TV, the Edge told *Pulse!* that it was the tour that had the biggest musical influence on *Zooropa*.

Zooropa represented U2 pushing themselves away from their 1980s American-influenced sound even further than they did for *Achtung Baby*. It is an album that musically and conceptually reaches deeper into the European aesthetic that had inspired them. *Zooropa*'s harder technological edge is captured throughout the album, with songs like 'Daddy's Gonna Pay for Your Crashed Car' and 'Dirty Day' finding the groove within its industrial rock rhythms.

Even some of the album's singles were daring demonstrations of U2's emphasis on experimentation. 'Numb' – the album's first single which originated from an *Achtung Baby* out-take called 'Down All the Days' – showcases U2's seamless use of samples as a means to recreate the sensory overload sensation of Zoo TV. 'Numb' also features the Edge on lead vocals delivering lines in a rap-like monotone, with Bono relegated to the background singing falsetto. Bono's falsetto singing style, often referred to as his 'Fat Lady' voice due to its operatic melodrama, comes to the forefront on 'Lemon', *Zooropa*'s second single and a disco-driven track that resulted in several dance mixes.

U2 had not only advanced musically on *Zooropa*, but lyrically as well, as the tour's concept shifted the songwriting to become more philosophical. A song about a man's obsessive need to control the celebrity he sees on television, 'Babyface' exhibits U2's musical playfulness. With songs like 'Some Days Are Better Than Others', with its juxtaposing bass-driven cool and jangly trippiness, and 'The First Time', with lyrics reinterpreting the prodigal son as not returning home, these take the band's inner turmoil and add emotional depth to the album.

The album's opening track, 'Zooropa',

The Edge at the 10th Annual MTV Video Music Awards at the Universal Amphitheatre, California, 1993.

imagines a surrealistic vision of a futuristic Europe. Combining U2's studio and soundcheck recordings, and featuring lyrics directly pulled from advertising slogans, 'Zooropa' gives the album a setting. Inspired by the work of cyberpunk author William Gibson, Bono envisioned the song to signify the neon-lit metropolis as the conceptual landscape in which the rest of the album, *Zooropa*, is based.

Closing the album is 'The Wanderer', a collaboration between U2 and Johnny Cash that came about when Bono convinced Cash to come into the studio while Cash was in Dublin for another gig. The country-music legend – a year before his career comeback with the Rick Rubin-produced *American Recordings* – provided lead vocals as the song's narrator, a preacher who sets out with his Bible and gun in what he sees as a spiritually dystopic wasteland. According to Flood, it is one of the highlights of the album, *Zooropa*, for its sonic experimentation translating the emotional brilliance of the song. 'If you imagine the album being set in this place, Zooropa,' said Flood, '… it throws a whole different light on the conceptualization of the record.'

Amidst all the industrial and electronic experimentation, 'Stay (Faraway, So Close!)' is a standout track on *Zooropa* and is among U2's favourite recorded songs. The song was inspired by Frank Sinatra, though more emotionally rather than musically. While U2 were recording *Zooropa*, Bono joined Sinatra for a rerecording of 'I've Got You Under My Skin' for Sinatra's 1993 *Duets* album after Sinatra told him, 'You are the only man with an earring I am going to like.' A more guitar and drum heavy mix was used in the Wim Wenders film *Faraway, So Close!* and was nominated for Best Original Song – Motion Picture at the 1993 Golden Globes.

Though it did not achieve the commercial and critical success of *Achtung Baby*, *Zooropa* hit its mark. It sold well enough to become another number one album for U2 and Zoo TV became

A performance group called the Massive Heeds, a warm-up act during the Zoo TV Tour.

the highest-grossing tour of its time, consisting of 157 shows across five legs from February 1992 through December 1993. While critics did not praise it as much as its predecessor, Zoopra earned positive reviews and won the 1994 Grammy Award for Best Alternative Music Album.

All things considered, U2 in the mid-1990s still enjoyed cultural relevance even after almost losing it not long before. Coming off a highly successful tour supporting two celebrated albums, it made sense to keep expanding in that direction. Going into 1994, the band were looking to take some time to refresh and relax, but also find ways to improve themselves professionally and personally. Adam had begun to lose control of his life due to alcohol abuse, which was affecting him so much that he was too hung-over to play the first concert in Sydney towards the end of Zoo TV, and guitar technician Stuart Morgan stepped in to take his place.

Adam left briefly with Larry to get clean in New York, where the two took time to study music production and programming. They also worked together on bass and percussion for several songs on Nanci Griffith's 1994 album *Flyer* and later composed the theme for the 1996 film *Mission: Impossible*. Bono and the Edge, who were spending more time with family, also continued working, recording 'North and South of the River' with Christy Moore and writing the theme song Tina Turner performed for the 1995 James Bond film *GoldenEye*. The band even contributed 'Hold Me, Thrill Me, Kiss Me, Kill Me' to the *Batman Forever* soundtrack, an unfinished track from *Zooropa* that earned U2 their second Golden Globe nomination.

By the end of 1994, the band were hitting a creative roadblock once again, but they were in a much better place than before. Brian Eno encouraged them to improvise to loosen up, as he had done since first collaborating with them on *The Unforgettable Fire*. When U2 were ready to start recording, they did not have any specific plan after a project had fallen through, which

was composing the soundtrack for the 1996 film *The Pillow Book* written and directed by Peter Greenaway. Looking to tap into that energy, and push them to experiment through improvisation more, Eno urged them to continue recording soundtrack contributions but for imaginary films.

The recording sessions would result in *Original Soundtracks 1*, an album collaboration between U2 and Eno under the pseudonym Passengers, released on 6 November 1995. Not having their name on the cover freed U2 from pressure over album sales. This led to the idea of using the album to parody the movie soundtracks saturating the market. The music came together through improvisational jamming, with Eno playing a bigger role than before, and created a diverse array of mostly instrumental compositions for films that did not exist, with the exception of three films that included *Ghost in the Shell* and *Beyond the Clouds*. The third real contribution, the film *Miss Sarajevo*, became the album's single. A song about a beauty pageant held during the siege of Sarajevo, 'Miss Sarajevo' is most notable for its guest vocals contributed by Italian tenor Luciano Pavarotti, a collaboration Bono calls his most beloved U2 song. The Passengers album flopped commercially compared with U2's proper albums, but had mixed reviews within the band. Larry said, 'There's a line between interesting music and self-indulgence. We crossed it on the Passengers record.'

U2 still wanted to go down the rabbit hole of experimentation after the Passengers album, but more towards dance music. Flood was brought back again as a producer and was joined by two new voices in the studio, Scottish DJ Howie B and British producer Nellee Hooper, though

Above: Children Of Bosnia Charity Concert. L-R: Brian Eno, Bono, The Edge and Luciano Pavarotti, Italy, 1995. Following spread: U2 promote the new PopMart Tour, New York, 1997

Hooper would not stay behind the console long and thus forfeited credit. Rehearsals for a new album began in mid-1995 shortly after the Passengers sessions, with the band practising in France and London before moving to Hanover Quay in Dublin. However, they did not end up with fully formed ideas. The band was also hindered by Larry suffering a back injury which forced them to reconsider how they developed songs together as a group. Instead of waiting for Larry to fully heal, U2 continued recording without him.

Larry did not appreciate the rest of the band working without him, so he spent his time during the sessions in February 1996 rerecording human replacements for the drum loops Howie mixed. This created a tense atmosphere, but things loosened up soon after getting more familiarized with working together using samples. Flood recalls that they especially found it more difficult working with their own samples than they did with other people's, a change he says was necessary to keep them from becoming artistically lazy. 'They're an uncomplicated way to get the ball rolling, but you're always in danger of sounding like some basic samples with the band on top. You're in danger of being dictated to by what's there, rather than saying: "This is just our springboard."'

Beyond using samples, Howie also challenged U2 to apply this to their songwriting process and how they played together. 'We took what we had and got the band to play to it and work it into their own idiom, while incorporating a dance ethic,' said Flood. These were learning experiences for U2, but they would soon become difficulties as time constraints became worse.

Confident they could finish the new album and release it in time for the 1996 Christmas shopping season, U2 agreed to schedule their next tour so they could promote it with shows beginning a few months later in April 1997. However, this would prove to be a critical mistake as U2 overestimated how much progress they were making in the studio.

As with *Zooropa*, U2 ended up with a lot of material. They were having difficulty finishing songs and were not really satisfied with them when they did, struggling to find a balance between songwriting and dance music. The creative wall forced them to delay the album's release to March 1997, giving them only a month to rehearse the new material before the tour started. The band kept recording with the deadline fast approaching, turning in the material so late that they scrambled to remix songs even as the album was being mastered. The Edge considered the final album as one created through compromise, recalling in *U2 by U2* that there was something inherently wrong since they could not mix it properly. Larry said not enough time was spent on the material and that the entire album would have been different if they were able to spend a few more months working.

Released on 3 March 1997, *Pop* furthered U2's musical reinvention that began with *Achtung Baby* and evolved during *Zooropa*. A bolder and darker take on techno and electronic dance music, with an emphasis on funkier rhythms and heavier effects processing, *Pop* is U2's experimentalism at its most frenetic. While critics were generally positive and the album sold rather well, enough to become the fifth consecutive number one album for U2 on the *Billboard* charts, U2 were disappointed with how the album turned out. So much so that they revisited the songs and eventually remixed several of them to their liking for their 2002 compilation *The Best of 1990–2000*. Since the album had been rushed due to their touring obligations, Bono called it 'the most expensive demo session in the history of music'.

The rougher aesthetic of U2's experimentation surfaces throughout the album. 'Mofo', the most sonically aggressive song on *Pop*, is hard-hitting musically and thematically as a song about Bono grieving his mother. Another emotionally heavy but slower song, 'Do You Feel Loved' is an atypical love song with Bono asking a deep question but without actually turning it into one. On 'Gone', the Edge's brutally piercing guitar sounds like it came from a 1970s German experimental band, and is U2 responding to

critics who condemned them for becoming successful.

Pop continued to satirize the media, but more from the intersection of irony and celebrity culture. Making music influenced by what was happening in dance clubs, *Pop* also lyrically lampoons the culture by holding a mirror to its face. 'Last Night on Earth' – an album single with a music video that features model Sophie Dahl as well as author William S. Burroughs' final appearance on film – is a song about a woman partying her way down a path of self-destruction that came together towards the end of the recording sessions. The trip rock motif of 'Miami' is a hazy slideshow ode to the city's nightlife while 'The Playboy Mansion' relies on references to pop-culture icons to address spiritual yearning.

As *Pop*'s first single, 'Discothèque' combines all the best qualities of the album as its opener. The song's lyrics and music video, which shows the band dancing inside a mirror ball and dressed up like the Village People, echo the irony of Zoo TV as cultural commentary wrapped up in sequins and space disco.

While the serious themes behind some of the songs get overshadowed by the album's electronic adrenaline, it is the slower songs on *Pop* that reveal its complex diversity. One of the few songs with acoustic guitar on *Pop*, 'Staring at the Sun' is a snapshot of Bono's personal introspection at the time while 'If God Will Send His Angels' is him asking for divine help. 'If You Wear That Velvet Dress' – the song Nellee Hooper worked on with U2 very early in the *Pop* sessions before leaving and losing album credit – smoothly blends sex with spirituality. Despite beginning on a danceable note, *Pop* closes with the two most emotionally raw songs on the album, with 'Please' signifying a prayer for the peace process to end the Troubles in Ireland and Bono pleading for Jesus to save humanity on 'Wake Up Dead Man'.

Soon the challenge became how to support the album with a tour. Trying to recapture the size and scope of Zoo TV, but without repeating themselves, U2 crafted

Bono performs during the PopMart Tour in San Francisco, USA, 1997.

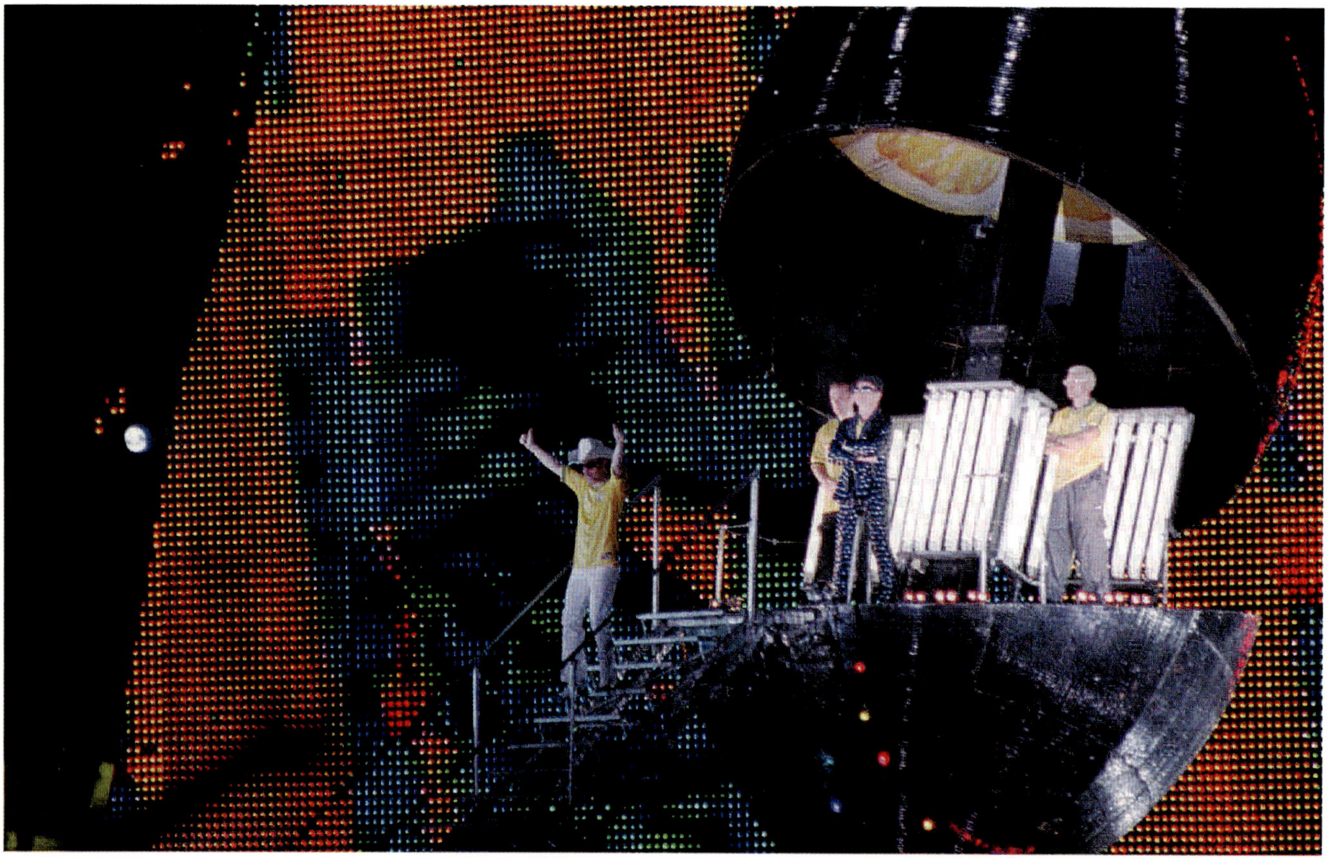

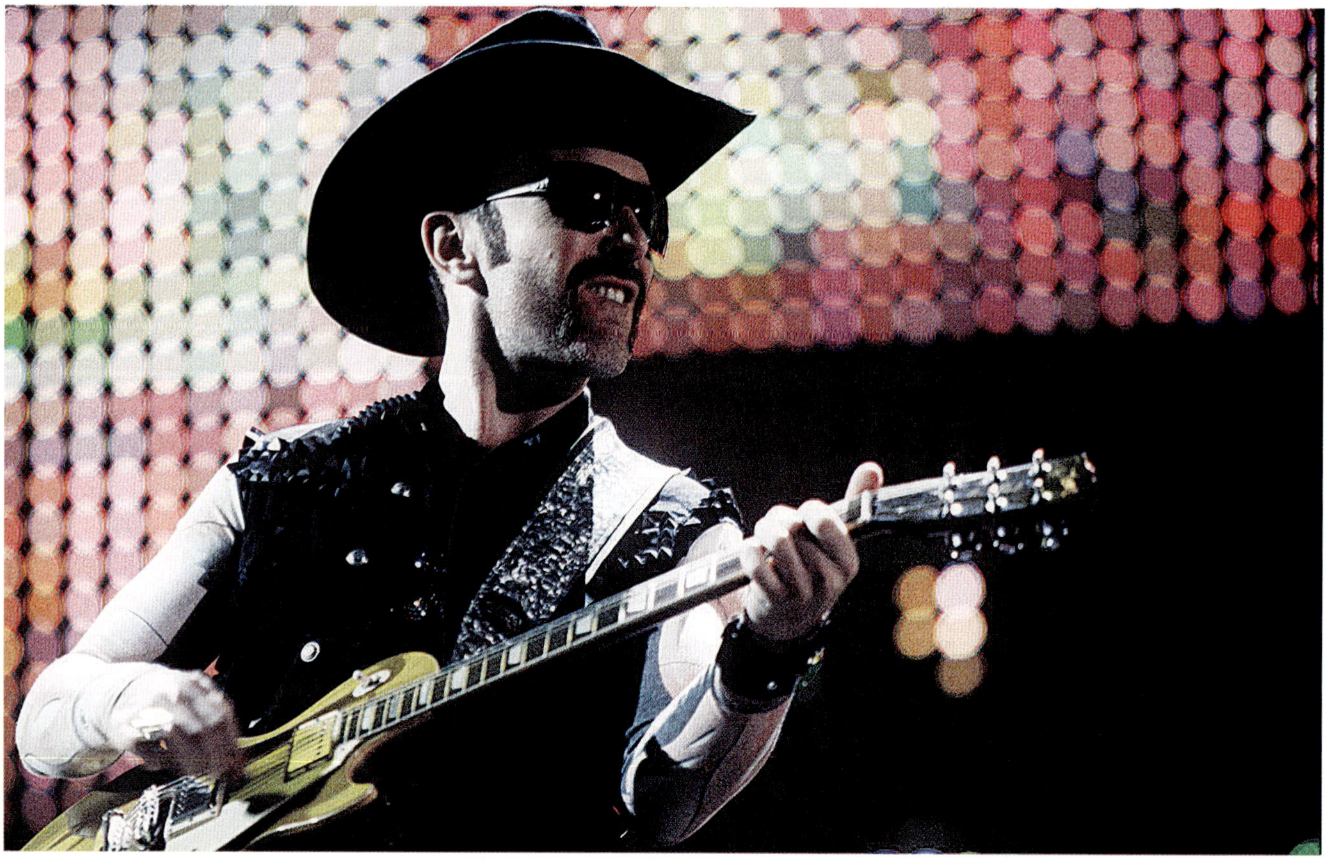

PopMart: Live From Mexico City as another monumental multimedia spectacle to channel and accentuate the artistic irony inherent within *Pop*. Instead of several dozen screens that each had their own video feed, PopMart featured a single 165-foot-wide LED screen opulently centred by a 100-foot-tall McDonald's-esque golden arch flanked by a giant mirror-ball lemon that slid down an olive-tipped cocktail stirrer. PopMart's stage and tour concept was meant to criticize mass consumerism and corporate worship, using its own imagery against them.

It was a concept U2 committed to from the very beginning of the tour, even turning its announcement into a type of performance art. U2 announced the tour for their new album from the sales floor of a Kmart discount store in Manhattan, revealing the tour details and following it up with a live performance of 'Holy Joe', the B-side to 'Discothèque', from the lingerie department. It was the moment when U2 began to blur the line between satire and reality, the start of something they are still not sure of themselves. 'I can't quite recall how it got to the idea of taking a supermarket on the road,' said Bono of PopMart. 'I remember it making a lot of sense at the time.'

Like Zoo TV did for *Achtung Baby* and *Zooropa*, PopMart turned the excess on *Pop* up to the highest level. The cultural commentary on celebrity and capitalism transformed the satire into a Warholian Frankenstein display of mass music conglomeration, with U2's ironic intention coming off as arrogant and out of touch. At the beginning of each show, Bono would come out swinging with pop-star swagger, quite literally, surrounded by bodyguards and throwing punches like a boxer. As the band took to the stage, advancing a key visual component from Zoo TV, the massive widescreen rapidly flashed pop-culture icons. Towards the end, a sheet would fall off to reveal a giant mirror ball, turning the PopMart encore into a dance club as the band emerges from the lemon and descended back on to the stage. 'It's trying to be humorous about the position we find ourselves in as a big band playing big stadiums,' said the Edge. 'We take the music seriously, but we're able to try to laugh at the sheer commercial size of what we're undertaking.'

PopMart became a challenging experience for U2. The stage design and production, while innovative, was also sensitive and complicated. Technical issues would sometimes occur, including U2 getting stuck in the lemon on two separate occasions before going out to perform. The band were also under-rehearsed due to the delayed release of *Pop*, apparent during their performance on the tour's opening night in Las Vegas on 25 April 1997, a concert that Carter Alan said was the worst U2 show he had ever seen. Though their performance improved throughout the first leg across the United States, their spirits dampened as reviews rechristened their tour as 'FlopMart' and ticket sales were low.

When U2 set out on the second leg in Europe during July 1997, they had a better grasp of the material and earned critical praise for the shows. The songs were sounding better, but they still could not bear the weight of the tour, with Larry saying in *U2 by U2* that the problem with PopMart was that *Pop* was not big enough to support its concept. With fewer than 100 shows due to its size and expense, PopMart concluded during March 1998 with U2's first concerts in South Africa, less than a year after it began.

Despite the conceptual irony, a couple of shows during PopMart turned the mass media spectacle towards political activism. While in Europe for Zoo TV during the summer of 1993, U2 were introduced to Bill Carter, a documentary filmmaker turned aid worker who was capturing the carnage of the Bosnian War and the siege of Sarajevo after paramilitary forces sieged the city following Bosnia and Herzegovina's independence from Yugoslavia. Carter told U2 about the people there who, as a form of therapy in their darkest hours, played music and built a scene to distract them from the horrors outside the makeshift bomb shelters they lived in. Carter also told U2 how their music was really important to the besieged Sarajevans. 'When I heard the music of U2 politically,' said Gino Jevdjevic, lead singer of Kulture Shock, in the documentary *Kiss the Future*, 'they represent something that I realized in this war … was a personification of our resistance.' Without the consent of the rest of the band, Bono promised Carter that U2 would raise awareness of the war in Sarajevo. As the rest of the band feared that the negative publicity would overshadow their efforts, U2 did not

Opposite top: U2 emerge from a giant lemon during the PopMart Tour in Rio de Janeiro, 1998.
Opposite bottom: The Edge in San Diego, 1997.
Following spread: Soundcheck during the PopMart Tour, Arizona, 1997.

go to Sarajevo during Zoo TV, instead using satellite communications for Bono to remotely interview Carter onstage and to show a human side of the war he felt had gone unnoticed by the mass media.

The opportunity to rally support behind Sarajevans with a concert came up again during PopMart when, at a loss of half a million pounds, U2 took the full PopMart experience to war-torn Sarajevo for a concert on 23 September 1997. With how much the messaging of their music meant to the people, U2 felt it was important to treat Sarajevo with the same dignity as any other city on the tour. The crew transported the stage across the country and hired several hundred locals to help assemble it, with U2 setting up offices in the shell-damaged Zetra Olympic Hall and staying in a hotel with mortar-punctured walls and floors. It was such a significant event for Sarajevo that trains became operational for the first time since the start of the war, with over 45,000 people in attendance and openers including local bands Protest and Sikter as well as the Islamic Gazi Husrev-Beg high school choir. The concert validated the lives and dignity of the people affected by the war, with local press calling the day after 'the day the siege of Sarajevo ended.' A local student said, 'I felt excluded from the world for so long. It's not only about U2. It's the feeling of being part of the world.'

'The fact that we can come and put on, not just a concert, but the same concert that we've put on in Paris, New York and London, I think is maybe a symbol for the people of Sarajevo that things are getting back to normal,' said the Edge.

Several months later, beginning in January 1998, U2 took PopMart to South America. On 11 February U2 played in Santiago, their first show in Chile, which was broadcast live to the entire country. They performed at the Estadio Nacional which had previously been a prison camp following the 1973 *coup d'état* conducted by dictator Augusto Pinochet. Following a performance of 'One', with nearly every eye in the country on them, U2 closed the concert with 'Mothers of the Disappeared' while inviting Chilean mothers to come onstage and hold photographs of their missing children, symbolically demanding their government to tell them what had happened to their loved ones. Bono made a direct plea to Pinochet on the broadcast, saying, 'Tell them where their children are so they can bury them, so they can say goodbye to them, so Chile can say goodbye to the past. God is your judge. Please, give the dead back to the living.' Despite the spectacle of the tour, U2 could still tap into the heart of their music and use their platform to make a socially conscious statement that had a deeply significant meaning.

U2 had journeyed so far into America during the 1980s that they almost lost their way back home, and what they found upon their return to Europe opened a new world of musical discovery for them throughout the 1990s. With the image of what they had become by the end of the decade, whether it all became a misunderstood art project or whether the irony was really beginning to wear thin, U2 had run the risk of once again becoming caricatures of themselves. U2's path through the 1990s was lit by the glow of neon signs, but even nightclubs have to close eventually, leaving them to stumble out of the afterparty and into the twilight. Though, they would not have to wander long, because with the dawn of a new millennium came the early rays of a bright new beautiful day.

4

Beautiful
Day

U2 had a lot to be grateful for by the end of the 1990s

, especially considering how differently things could have gone a decade earlier had they not chosen to risk stepping out of their comfort zone. It was a creatively rich decade, with U2 going through major artistic and personal changes, but it was time to put away the masks and rediscover who they were. Going into a new millennium, filled with joy, U2 reinvented themselves again by returning to their roots: the heart and soul of what made them a band.

Shortly after PopMart, Bono began experiencing difficulty with his voice due to a growth on his vocal cords that caused them to swell. U2 were set to begin recording their next album but his voice was too weak, so he went to consult a surgeon. In *U2 by U2*, Bono recalls being terrified by having to get a biopsy, worrying that it would mean he would not be able to work on the album for several months and that his voice would be too unpractised for him to be any good in the studio. He also thought a lot about his own death. When the examination revealed a biopsy would not be needed, Bono felt a profound sense of relief that was life-changing because the threat of facing a serious illness forced him to appreciate what mattered most in his life. He was more than just a rock star. He was a husband and a father, a family man with people who loved and needed him. His childhood home was no longer peaceful after his mother died, which led to a combative relationship with his father, and Bono feared him dying would put his family through the same trauma. 'There is nothing like a brush with mortality to put things into perspective,' he said.

Bono wanted to bring an enlightened outlook to U2's next album, breaking away from the conceptualized irony of art and celebrity to instead look inward at the joy of living. In *Surrender*, Bono recalls speaking with Brian Eno about producing the album, saying, 'Let's make every single song something you can't live without … let's make an album of essential communications.' Eno suggested that the album could sound more personal if it were thought of as a musical memory book. Describing his album vision as 'The conversations you can't not have, the pictures you must take with you when you leave, our interpersonal relationships,'

Bono felt U2 could make music that expressed the complexities of that vulnerability with honesty and joy.

When U2 went into Hanover Quay Studios in late 1998 to begin recording demos with Eno and Daniel Lanois, they were already a world away from PopMart despite the tour just ending a few months earlier. The Edge told *Rolling Stone* that the creative direction behind *Pop* allowed U2 to take 'the idea of deconstructing things as far as we could', but it also made them realize they were 'losing certain key aspects of what a rock 'n' roll band is supposed to be'. The Edge wanted U2 to refocus on their instruments as the band's core.

'We absolutely wanted to showcase the chemistry of a band,' said the Edge. 'But in so doing, we bumped into the opposite problem occasionally, which is that rock 'n' roll bands tend to sound samey.' To help U2 avoid sounding monotonous, Eno encouraged them to record a lot of music quickly, instead of developing ideas outside the studio, and then choosing the best material for the album. Despite three weeks of jamming, not much came from the sessions, but the mood in the studio was still positive and supportive. The Edge said Eno and Lanois 'kept things sounding really unique even though it was very much a band record.' However, one memorable moment during the demo session left them feeling especially inspired – during a jam, Bono's voice returned and he hit a high note that he had been unable to reach for a decade.

The band remained confident they could release an album the following year in 1999. After the demo sessions ended, the Edge continued working on song ideas. The songwriting process had become important for him. He told *Rolling Stone* that *Pop* lacked a song that 'really connected with people' because 'the songwriting really took a back seat to the experimentation'. In *U2 by U2*, he added that U2 were spending more time on songwriting than they had before. The idea for those earlier albums was that by developing the song through improvisational jamming, he said U2 could avoid the clichés associated with more traditional songwriting methods. However, now this was a craft they wished to hone.

Delays also affected U2's ability to develop

material, with recording affected by Bono not being around the studio as much. Bono had recently learned about Jubilee 2000, an international campaign advocating for the cancellation of Third World debt by 2000. Over the years since his first humanitarian trip to Africa in 1986, Bono had grown more aware of how Western governments kept African nations in debt through economic development loans that were squandered by corrupt leaders with their citizens left with the bill. It was an issue he took very seriously, so he swiftly jumped into action to support the Jubilee 2000 campaign, writing a February 1999 editorial for *The Guardian* called 'World Debt Angers Me' to increase public support.

Bono pushed for world leaders to support Jubilee 2000, such as lobbying members of Congress and even visiting Bill Clinton to get his support for debt cancellation. Bono also met with James D. Wolfensohn, the president of the World Bank, which had developed the Heavily Indebted Poor Countries initiative that provided low-interest loans to poverty-stricken countries, to put pressure on him and other creditors to eliminate the debt entirely. Leveraging his rock-star status, Bono joined 50,000 people at a protest outside the G8 summit in Cologne, Germany, where he handed German Chancellor Gerhard Schröder a petition signed by 17 million people calling for full debt relief. In September 1999, Jubilee 2000 gained a huge boost of awareness when Bono visited Pope John Paul II to get his papal blessing for debt relief. In *Surrender*, Bono recalls giving the Pope a copy of Seamus Heaney's *Collected Poems* and his blue-tinted wrap-around sunglasses, with him receiving rosary beads with a crucifix in return. The media coverage of their meeting bolstered huge support for Jubilee 2000. By the end of the month, Clinton declared the United States' commitment to fully forgive the debt, with Bono saying he heard the president rewrote his speech to the World Bank while in the car on his way to meet with them. Soon other countries followed, resulting in $100 billion in cancelled debt due to Bono's advocacy.

Recording the album was also delayed by another music project. While making *Rattle and Hum*, Bono had an early mental sketch for a movie while on the roof of the New Rosslyn Hotel in Los Angeles, also known as the Million Dollar Hotel, that started with a man

Opposite: The Verve's Richard Ashcroft and The Edge chat backstage at Live 8 London, 2005. The concerts preceded the G8 summit to raise awareness for Make Poverty History.
This page: Bono performing at the 2000 MTV Europe Music Awards in Sweden, 2000.

jumping from the roof of one building on to another. Bono collaborated with screenwriter Nicholas Klein to expand the idea into a script, which over a decade later became the 2000 Wim Wenders-directed film *The Million Dollar Hotel*. Recording for U2's new album was delayed for two months while Bono worked with Lanois and American music producer Hal Willner on the film's soundtrack. U2 recorded two songs for the soundtrack, which offered a sneak peek at the band-oriented post-*Pop* sound: 'Stateless' and the Salman Rushdie-penned 'The Ground Beneath Her Feet'. Bono and Lanois contributed to other songs on the soundtrack, joined by a group Willner put together called The Million Dollar Hotel Band that included jazz musicians such as Brad Mehldau and Bill Frisell, including 'Never Let Me Go', 'Falling At Your Feet' and a reprise of 'The First Time' from *Zooropa*.

During the recording sessions, there was an incident that was all too familiar to Bono. Similar to what happened before U2 recorded *October*, a laptop containing lyrics was stolen from Bono's car outside the Clarence Hotel in Dublin. Bono was soon reunited with the laptop after a man, who purchased it second-hand for £300, returned it after finding a picture of Bono's son on it. 'Everything I'd written since August was on this, and I hadn't backed up any of it,' said Bono, 'so I would really have been a goner.'

After two decades together, U2 realized their approach to making music had changed. While Eno and Lanois were frustrated that Bono was not focused on recording, the rest of U2 were unbothered by it. Adam said in *U2 by U2* that the band could take time to focus on the specifics of an idea without Bono, with the Edge saying that there were still ways for them to explore song ideas even though they were not playing together as much. Larry agreed that Bono's absence did not hinder the rest of the band's creativity, adding that everyone had families outside the band which helped take the pressure off in the studio. In *Surrender*, Bono said the time he dedicated to his activism 'turned music … into what I did on my days off'. Due to his attention

being pulled elsewhere and yearning to get back to his first love of making music, Bono felt sharply present during the recording sessions and was filled with joy whenever he was there. 'To be back in the studio became something I craved,' Bono said.

U2 also had a very practical reason for not stressing over recording delays. With *Pop*, scheduling conflicts forced U2 to release an album they considered unfinished. They were not looking to make the same mistake again, so they painstakingly worked on the new album throughout 1999 at Windmill Lane Studios, Westland Studios, Totally Wired Studios and even in their homes in the South of France.

Released on 30 October 2000, *All That You Can't Leave Behind* was a new U2 for a new age. Debuting on the charts at number one in 32 countries, *All That You Can't Leave Behind* was a massive commercial success for U2 and would become their fourth bestselling album ever. In addition to the public being won over by U2's musical return to grace, the critics also praised U2 for getting back to basics, lauding them for how intimate and personal their music had become. It won seven Grammy Awards, including Song of the Year in 2001 and Best Rock Album in 2002, and is still the only album to earn two Record of the Year winning singles over two years. Since its release, *All That You Can't Leave Behind* is not only considered one of U2's best albums, but also one of the best albums of the 2000s.

The love of life that Bono wanted to infuse into the songs can be heard throughout *All That You Can't Leave Behind*, the most notable being 'Beautiful Day' which became a massive hit. As both the album's opener and first single, 'Beautiful Day' was an emotionally powerful creative statement to listeners and critics who felt that U2 had lost their way. The song originated from an earlier track called 'Always' that later became a B-side. The song was proving difficult to record, with the rock approach sounding too bare. Frustrated with their lack of progress, Eno created a drum machine rhythm and added piano and

Previous spread: U2 visit Radio 1 studios in Maida Vale to promote *All That You Can't Leave Behind*, London, 2000
Opposite: Bono and The Edge during the Elevation Tour, Netherlands, 2001.

synthesized strings over it, with Lanois and the Edge then adding guitars. In *Surrender*, Bono recalls being astonished at how much it sounded like U2. Twenty minutes into the jam, Bono sang the lines 'It's a beautiful day / Don't let it get away' which were then edited out and later formed the chorus for 'Beautiful Day'. Bono described the song as being about a man who finds joy in what he still has after losing everything.

'Wild Honey', a light-hearted track that also expressed joy, was a bit of an anomaly that seemed out of place musically for U2. Bono strongly pushed for the song to be on the album, saying it would playfully break up the mood of the album. The song also had its support outside the band, with Eno enjoying it, thinking it was based on Van Morrison, and Lanois saying, 'We thought it would be fun to include it; a nice, simple, clear song with a lovely sentiment'.

'Walk On' was written about Aung San Suu Kyi, who had been under house arrest since 1989 for pro-democracy activities in Burma, which is now Myanmar. Bono was inspired by her resilience and wrote the song from the perspective of standing up for what is right in the face of great sacrifice, calling it 'one of the great acts of the twentieth century'. Due to 'Walk On', Myanmar banned *All That You Can't Leave Behind*, declaring that anyone who owned the album would face up to 20 years in prison. The liner notes dedicated the song to Suu Kyi, but this later changed when her house arrest ended in 2010 and she defended the Myanmar military's ethnic cleansing of the Rohingya people, which resulted in her arrest following a *coup d'état* in 2021. For the 20th anniversary reissue of *All That You Can't Leave Behind*, 'Walk On' is now dedicated to the 'Rohingya people whose human rights have been so persistently and brutally denied'.

Bono wanted the album to really showcase his singing. When his voice returned during the demo sessions, it was while singing the line 'I'm a man / I'm not a child' which are heard later in 'Kite', the only song idea from the demo sessions to make it on to the final album. Bono's vocal performance elevates the song's lyrics and themes, which were inspired by an afternoon flying kites with his daughters until they told him they wanted to go back home and play with their Tamagotchi virtual pets. Bono described the song as about the

act of letting go in a relationship with the kite representing something beyond your control. Other songs on *All That You Can't Leave Behind* demonstrate Bono's vocals in more subtle ways that explore how experience has shaped his style as a performer. With lyrics addressed to his wife Ali, Bono performed the vocals for 'In a Little While' during two improvisational takes while hung-over and having only slept two hours.

While many perceived *All That You Can't Leave Behind* as U2 going back to their earlier anthemic sound from the 1980s, they actually brought with them sonic elements from *Pop* to further evolve and craft their new sound. 'Elevation' opens with a distorted electronic effect and features a rhythm that came from Adam's appreciation of hip-hop. The song was issued as a single with a harder and funkier mix produced for the soundtrack to the 2001 film *Lara Croft: Tomb Raider*. On 'New York', a song that originated from a drum loop pattern by Larry and which was pieced together from various performances, U2 seamlessly merge their electronic and rock qualities.

While there is a lot of joy throughout *All That You Can't Leave Behind*, there is also some pain. As Adam told *Rolling Stone*, the album was 'about the journey we'd been through as a band, as men in relationships, as sons of mothers and fathers. It was about the baggage that you have to live with, the sense of loss'. A song that started out as a gospel-influenced chord progression from the Edge, 'Stuck in a Moment You Can't Get Out Of' was written by Bono about the 1997 suicide of his friend, INXS lead singer Michael Hutchence, delivering a one-sided argument telling Hutchence how foolish he was. In *Surrender*, Bono remembers his close relationship with Hutchence becoming strained due to his substance-abuse issues, reflecting on the song's narrator as sounding intolerant and 'not as forgiving as he should be'.

'Peace on Earth' and 'When I Look at the World' both explore loss in more abstract ways. 'Peace on Earth' was written about the Omagh car bombing in Northern Ireland on 15 August 1998, where a Provisional Irish Republican Army group killed 29 people and injured 220 more in opposition to the Good Friday Agreement that ended most of the violence of the Troubles. Bono called it 'the lowest day of my life'. Tired of all the

Oppostie: Michael Hutchence of INXS, 1990.

promises to cease the bloodshed, Bono asks the question, 'So what's it worth? / This peace on Earth', a world-weary sentiment not unlike the spirit of 'Sunday Bloody Sunday' demanding an answer to how long must we sing this song. 'When I Look at the World' explores how someone questions their faith in the face of tragedy, echoing the feeling of 'Peace on Earth'.

'Grace' closes the album and captures U2's hope for a better world. In *U2 by U2*, Bono explains that grace is his favourite word because it evokes forgiveness as an act of love. Bono says that while mistakes result in consequences, having grace take away those burdens is a concept that can change the world. In the spirit of *All That You Can't Leave Behind*, it signifies the joy that comes from not having to bear the burden of emotional baggage.

During his Grammy acceptance speech for 'Beautiful Day' winning Song of the Year, Bono said, 'We're back, reapplying for the job of best band in the world', which U2 would set to prove on tour. Just like they did for *All That You Can't Leave Behind*, U2 scaled things back for the Elevation Tour. Instead of large multimedia stadium shows, U2 simplified the stage design down to the essentials for more intimate indoor arena concerts. In addition to the main stage, a heart-shaped catwalk extended 100 feet out into the audience, creating an enclosed area for the audience within the heart. Willie Williams, who has designed all U2's tours since 1983, designed the stage to allow the band to move around and create a closer connection with their fans, such as organizing seating in the round. Hanging above U2 were four screens that each showed raw footage of a different member, a creative decision Williams convinced U2 would be one of the most memorable elements of the tour. In *U2 by U2*, the band recalled how much they enjoyed playing indoors again and reminding audiences that *Pop* was over. They also rejected the notion that the tour was them getting back to their roots, with the Edge saying that it was all relative because both the tour and album used advanced technology but in more subtle ways. The Elevation Tour ran from March through December 2001, with 113 shows over three legs across North America and Europe. It also became the highest-grossing tour that year

and won several awards for its design and technical achievements.

All That You Can't Leave Behind and the Elevation Tour celebrated the joy in life, but that theme would take on a whole new meaning after tragedy struck. On 11 September 2001, al-Qaeda carried out a coordinated terrorist attack in the United States. It was the deadliest terrorist attack on United States soil and a devastating beginning to a new chapter in the nation's history.

Days after the attack, on 21 September, U2 participated in *America: A Tribute to Heroes*, a televised benefit concert that raised funds for the victims of the attacks and their families. It included performances from several dozen musicians, including Bruce Springsteen performing 'My City of Ruins', Neil Young covering John Lennon's 'Imagine' and a gospel choir backing Faith Hill singing 'There Will Come a Day'. Performing via satellite from London, U2 played a segment of 'Peace on Earth' that segued into 'Walk On' with them joined by Dave Stewart, formerly of Eurythmics, on guitar and Natalie Imbruglia and Morleigh Steinberg singing backing vocals.

The themes of *All That You Can't Leave Behind* began to really resonate with people after the attacks. The Edge told *Rolling Stone* in 2020, 'It takes on a life of its own. You never know how a song will be used, what value it'll have once it's out. It's mind-blowing to see how some of these songs became so much of the moment and how they connected with people in such a powerful way.' Bono echoed this, saying, 'You're never the author of your success anyway, but fate really took the album and changed those songs.'

When U2 began their final leg of the Elevation Tour in the United States during October 2001, the concerts took on a more emotional tone. In *Rolling Stone*, the Edge recalls U2 bringing first responders onstage during their three nights performing at Madison Square Garden in New York to share their stories and pay tribute to those who lost their lives.

Janet Jackson was originally scheduled to perform the half-time show at Super Bowl XXXVI in New Orleans on 3 February 2002, but cancelled after the 11 September attacks. Since the attacks were still fresh in the national consciousness, the National Football

Previous spread: Photo shoot in Los Angeles, 2001.
Opposite: U2 accept the Grammy for Record of the Year for 'Beautiful Day', 2001.
Following page: Bono and former US President George W. Bush, Washington, 2002.

League (NFL) sought out a different artist that would better fit the sombre mood of the game, choosing U2 because of how they addressed the tragedy at the Madison Square Garden concerts. NFL spokesperson Brian McCarthy said, 'We certainly like the music, but we like the message that U2 carries, which is responsibility to others and a sense of freedom.' During the press conference announcing U2 as the new half-time show performance, Bono said, 'The whole year that we've had in the United States has really been extraordinary … and I suppose that post-September 11th, to have our album mean so much to people who are not U2 fans has made this year really special for us, and to be at the Super Bowl, and to know that this is the very heart of America, I think it feels right for us to be here.'

On a heart-shaped stage modelled after the one used for the Elevation Tour, U2 opened the half-time show with 'Beautiful Day' for its resonance as a post-9/11 anthem. They then performed 'MLK' before segueing into 'Where the Streets Have No Name', all while a scrim raised behind the stage and projected a scrolling list featuring names of the attack victims. At the end, Bono opened his leather jacket to reveal an American flag lining as a statement of solidarity that capped an emotionally uplifting experience. 'Even if you're not American,' said Bono, 'everyone became an American that day.'

Before U2 began recording *All That You Can't Leave Behind* in 1998, they also began to reflect on their legacy. That year they released their first greatest hits album *The Best of 1980–1990*, which was supported by 'Sweetest Thing', a rerecorded version of a B-side from *The Joshua Tree* that they released as a single. After the success of *All That You Can't Leave Behind*, U2 followed with their second greatest hits album *The Best of 1990–2000*. This included two new songs, 'Electrical Storm' and 'The Hands That Built America', the latter of which was written for the soundtrack to Martin Scorsese's 2002 film *Gangs of New York* and would go on to win Best Original Song at the 2003 Golden Globes and earn U2 their first Academy Award nomination.

Bono's profile as an activist was also growing during this time. In 2002, Bono met with George W. Bush to persuade the United States to provide financial support to African countries impacted by the AIDS epidemic. After their meeting, they both went to the Inter-American Development Bank where Bush requested that $5 billion in aid be provided. On his meeting with Bush, Bono said, 'It is much easier and hipper for me to be on the barricades with a handkerchief over my nose – it looks better on the résumé of a rock 'n' roll star. But I can do better by just getting into the White House and talking to a man who I believe listens, wants to listen, on these subjects.' The next year, in 2003, Bush authorized the President's Emergency Plan for AIDS Relief (PEPFAR) programme which would save approximately 17 million lives, saying that the legislation would never have passed without Bono's efforts, and awarded him the Medal for Distinguished Leadership.

In 2002, Bono also co-founded the non-profit organization DATA (Debt, AIDS, Trade, Africa) which focused on eliminating the AIDS epidemic and loosening trade burdens across Africa. To promote DATA's advocacy and relief programmes, Bono embarked on The Heart of America Tour, a seven-day speaking tour throughout the American Midwest during December 2002, joined by other celebrity activists like Chris Rock, Ashley Judd and Lance Armstrong. The tour was captured in a short documentary feature which premiered at the Tribeca Film Festival in May 2004.

In 2004, Bono co-founded the ONE campaign which raised public support for eliminating extreme poverty throughout Africa by lobbying governments to provide medical and economic aid. 'I'm going to spend the rest of my life on this,' said Bono. 'I'm going to make that kind of extreme poverty history.' Two years later, in 2006, Bono co-founded (RED), a brand that licensed various products, such as clothing and consumer electronics, to raise funds and awareness for the Global Fund to Fight AIDS, tuberculosis and malaria.

In 2003, U2 participated in the opening ceremony of the 11th Special Olympics World Summer Games. Held in Croke Park in Dublin, it was the first time the Special Olympics were held outside the United States. U2 performed a two-song set, playing 'One', while accompanied by the RTÉ National Symphony Orchestra, and then 'Pride (In the Name of Love)', with Bono changing lines to include Nelson Mandela who later joined the band onstage.

When U2 went back into the studio to record a new album in February 2003, they wanted to continue the band-focused dynamic established during *All That You Can't Leave Behind*, but also focus on producing a harder rock sound while improving their songwriting. U2 reached back to their musical influences by listening to the artists that inspired them including, the Buzzcocks, Siouxsie and the Banshees and Echo & the Bunnymen. Wanting the album to sound like the bands they listened to growing up and to get a fresh voice in the studio, they reached out to Chris Thomas who had produced the Sex Pistols' *Never Mind the Bollocks: Here's the Sex Pistols*.

Unfortunately, Chris was unable to replicate the same magic with U2. Adam recalled in *U2 by U2* that Chris was becoming less comfortable producing the album as the sessions progressed, and that he was having a difficult time managing all U2's ideas because how they worked was less traditional than the other bands he produced.

After nine months of recording, U2 and Chris had produced enough songs to release an album, but doubt was growing among the band. Bono and the Edge felt the album was good and could be released in time for Christmas 2003, but Adam and Larry felt the songs lacked magic and that U2 should go back into the studio. 'On the last album there was lots of good feeling,' Adam said in *Time*, 'but only "Beautiful Day" was a hit. I felt that if our goal is still to be the biggest band in the world, the new record had to have three or four songs that would bring in new people. Three or four hits.'

With U2 split over whether to release the album, they asked Steve Lillywhite to listen to the songs and offer his opinion on what they should do. Feeling like the songs needed more work after listening to them, Lillywhite told *Time*, 'They played me the record and it was, well, it had the weight of the world on its shoulders. It certainly wasn't any fun,' After several lengthy discussions, Bono and the Edge were convinced the album should be shelved. 'The songs were good,' Bono said in *Time*, 'but good won't bring you to tears or make you want to leave your house and tour for a year. The bastards were right.' Chris was then given the bad news that U2 were not going to release the album he produced.

Sessions for a new album took place from

January through July 2004, with Lillywhite replacing Chris, his first time producing a U2 album since 1983's *War*. Since U2 already had a lot of material to work with, Lillywhite focused on helping them improve their playing, which the Edge said was helped by Lillywhite's positive attitude. Lillywhite also encouraged U2 to change their recording space, suggesting they use different rooms at Hanover Quay Studios because that would alter their playing and create a different sound. The Edge said that while some songs did not change much during these newer sessions, they did evolve because U2 were playing them better and were not stressing over ideas. 'They operate in total chaos,' said Lillywhite. 'They work slowly, get frustrated and then hold these epic meetings to bemoan how slowly they're working and how frustrated they are. I love them, but sometimes they just need to put one foot in front of the other.'

Four months after completing the album a second time with a new producer, U2 released *How to Dismantle an Atomic Bomb* on 22 November 2004. While it did not sell as many copies as *All That You Can't Leave Behind*, the new album debuted at number one in 34 countries which was two more than its predecessor. *How to Dismantle an Atomic Bomb* earned positive reviews upon release, most notably for its lyrical themes, though some critics felt U2 were playing it safe with their music by cultivating a more mainstream rock sound. However, *How to Dismantle an Atomic Bomb* was still a success for U2 artistically, being named the best album of 2004 by *USA Today*, *Paste* and the *New York Times*. It won eight Grammy Awards across two years, sweeping every category it was nominated for, including Song of the Year, Best Rock Album and Album of the Year in 2006. *How to Dismantle an Atomic Bomb* holds special significance for U2 with Bono and the Edge saying it represents their best songwriting and is what they think of as their best album.

Released as the lead single for *How to Dismantle an Atomic Bomb*, 'Vertigo' is the song that best captures the more sonically aggressive aesthetic U2 envisioned when they first went into the studio. The Edge's guitar drives 'Vertigo', with distortion used to great effect for the song's main power-chord riff and the ambient industrial drone that adds heft to the final chorus. The music came from a demo developed by the Edge while playing to a drum loop from Larry, with the melody evolving throughout the sessions. Bono then added lyrics, resulting in an early version of the song called 'Native Son', which was inspired by the conviction of Native American rights activist Leonard Peltier for the killing of two Federal Bureau of Investigation agents during a shootout on the Pine Ridge Indian Reservation in South Dakota on 26 June 1975. Many human rights activists like Nelson Mandela and the Dalai Lama campaigned for Peltier to be granted clemency. However, the lyrics were ultimately changed and the song retitled 'Vertigo'. On 'Native Son', Bono told *Rolling Stone*, 'The lyrics were about something I care deeply about, but the song didn't vibrate. It didn't change the temperature of the room.'

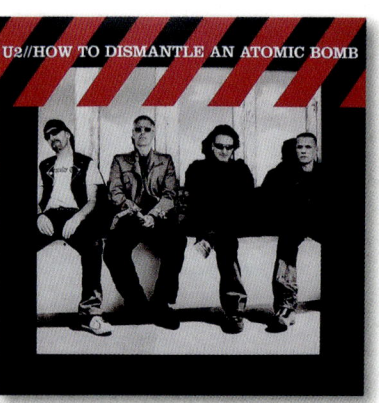

'Vertigo' became a huge hit after it was used in a television commercial for the Apple iPod, featuring U2 performing as silhouettes against solid-coloured backgrounds. The 'Vertigo' iPod commercial signified the beginning of U2's marketing partnership with Apple. In October 2004, U2 collaborated with Apple to release a special edition black-and-red U2-themed iPod. A month later, on 23 November 2004, U2 released the digital box set *The Complete U2* as an exclusive for Apple's iTunes Store. Compiling all U2's studio albums, singles and live albums to date, as well as including previously unreleased material, *The Complete U2* was the first digital set ever released.

During recording, the initial plan to make *How to Dismantle an Atomic Bomb* a more punk-influenced album gave way as songs evolved to cover themes such as family, intimacy and personal relationships. Bono's father, Bob Hewson, passed away from cancer in 2001, with Bono later writing about their

Previous spread: Nelson Mandela with The Edge and Bono, 2003. Opposite: Larry Mullen Jnr. shooting the video for *How to Dismantle an Atomic Bomb*, New York, 2003.

relationship for the song, 'Sometimes You Can't Make It On Your Own'. It had come from an earlier version called 'Tough', because Bono saw his father as a tough person who could be both charming and cynical, and Bono sang the song at his father's funeral. 'One Step Closer', also written by Bono about his dying father, was based on a conversation with Noel Gallagher of Oasis. Bono wondered if his father even believed in God, with Noel responding, 'Well, he's one step closer to knowing.'

Bono's activism also made its way into the music of the album. 'Crumbs From Your Table' is the most overtly political song, exploring the economic disparity experienced in developing countries due to the West's socio-economic power. In the song, Bono expresses his belief that where you live should not determine whether you live, a reflection of his involvement with organizations like DATA.

Though its narrative is not directly political, 'Miracle Drug' draws parallels between Bono's youth and his life as an adult. The lyrics were written about Bono's former schoolmate at Mount Temple, Irish author Christopher Nolan, who had been quadriplegic since birth due to his cerebral palsy. However, he gained the ability to communicate messages using a pointer attached to his forehead and would later publish several books, with critics comparing him to W. B. Yeats and James Joyce. Bono yearns for a miracle drug in the song's chorus, a desire that speaks to Nolan's experience but also becomes a plea in the context of Bono's activism to fight AIDS.

'Love And Peace Or Else' blends the theme of relationships with the fiery energy of Bono's politics. Wrapped in political imagery, the song is a passionate argument between lovers with Bono calling for a truce to end the fighting.

Other songs about relationships are more straightforward. Influenced by Phil Lynott's singing style, 'A Man and a Woman' is about rediscovering romance. 'Original of the Species,' evolved during *How to Dismantle an Atomic Bomb* to have a more adult tone, with Bono changing the lyrics to be about the erotic tension of knowing the difference between knowledge and wisdom.

Many of these themes also intersect with the album's spirituality as well. In *U2 by U2*, Bono says 'All Because of You,' another song

rooted in hard rock, is about reinventing yourself and being free of your mistakes. It is a song that carries dual meanings, one praising salvation through Jesus and the other honouring the musical heroes who inspired the members of U2 to create a band. 'Yahweh', the song that closes the album and is one of the few that Chris Thomas recorded, is about spiritual cleansing and having a relationship with God.

'City Of Blinding Lights' has since become one of the album's most beloved tracks. The earliest version of the song formed while recording *Pop* and was partially inspired by Bono's first trip to London before being changed to be about New York City following the 11 September attacks. By the time U2 were recording *How to Dismantle an Atomic Bomb*, 'City of Blinding Lights' had evolved to represent different personal ideas for Bono and has since become one of U2's modern concert staples. 'City of Blinding Lights' would gain further significance when President Barack Obama, who considers it one of his favourite songs, used it to announce his candidacy for the presidency in 2007 and again later in 2008 when he gave his acceptance speech at the Democratic National Convention in Denver, Colorado. Along with 'Pride (In the Name of Love)', U2 performed 'City Of Blinding Lights' at the We Are One concert at the Lincoln Memorial on 18 January 2009 to commemorate President Obama's forthcoming presidential inauguration.

U2 took the album out on the road for the Vertigo Tour. Much like the Elevation Tour, the stage design for the Vertigo Tour was stripped down to create a more intimate experience between U2 and the audience. A half-moon shaped catwalk extended from the stage, creating a B-stage that wrapped itself around a small portion of the audience closest to the main stage. While the stage designs between the Elevation Tour and the Vertigo Tour were relatively similar visually, the technology had advanced for the Vertigo Tour with the video screens replaced with retractable LED-based beaded curtains that hung down and displayed graphics and videos.

Though the production was scaled down in a similar way to the Elevation Tour, the Vertigo Tour was a bigger tour with 131 shows held across five legs from March 2005 through December 2006. In North America, shows were staged in indoor arenas like they were for the entirety of the Elevation Tour, but were expanded to outdoor stadiums internationally. The Vertigo Tour was a commercial success for U2, becoming the second highest grossing tour ever behind The Rolling Stones' A Bigger Bang Tour.

Even while touring, U2 were in a place in their career where they could look back on their own legacy. The Vertigo Tour was the first tour since 1989's Lovetown Tour where U2 played a song from every album they had released, including songs they rarely played live, as well as more obscure songs from their catalogue. Along with playing their more well-known hits, the Vertigo Tour was a space for U2 to showcase the range of their careers as artists. In *U2 by U2*, Adam said he felt U2 were revisiting the innocence of boyhood through the lens of their maturity as grown men.

The Vertigo Tour also became a space where Bono's politics entered the spotlight. For the Vertigo Tour, Bono said in *U2 by U2* that the band was looking to find the intersection between their personal lives and the bigger issues in the world. Bono became drawn to a piece of graffiti by Polish artist Piotr Młodożeniec called COEXIST, which featured an Islamic moon as the 'C', an 'X' for the Star of David and a 'T' to represent the Christian cross. For Bono, COEXIST became a symbol to address in concert the ongoing human rights abuses that were happening around the world. During the more political songs in the set, Bono would wear a COEXIST headband and address the audience, using it as an opportunity to rally support for initiatives like the ONE campaign. However, his bandmates were not as enthusiastic about the politics taking up space in the setlist. In *U2 by U2*, Larry said it was a struggle to balance the politics with the songs, with the Edge adding that Bono's lectures were not his favourite moments on tour, though they liked it when older songs held a contemporary political relevance.

The Vertigo Tour was prominently featured in U2's 2008 concert film *U2 3D*, their second feature film since 1988's *Rattle and Hum*. U2 filmed nine concerts in 2006 using 18 revolutionary 3D cameras to create a unique concert-film experience that became the first

Previous spread: L-R: A&M Records Chairman Jimmy Iovine, Bono, Steve Jobs and The Edge at a celebration of the release of a new Apple iPod family of products, California, 2004.

live-action digital 3D film. *U2 3D* premiered at the 2008 Sundance Film Festival and earned universal acclaim, becoming one of the highest-grossing concert films ever.

By the Vertigo Tour, U2 were being recognized for their musical legacy. In 2005, they were inducted into the Rock & Roll Hall of Fame during their first year of eligibility, and were joined by fellow inductees including The Pretenders, Percy Sledge, Buddy Guy and The O'Jays. Bruce Springsteen, whom Bono inducted in 1999, inducted U2, describing them as 'keepers of some of the most beautiful sonic architecture in rock 'n' roll' and saying they 'carried their faith in the great inspirational and resurrective power of rock 'n' roll'. During his induction speech, the Edge said, 'Above all else, what U2 have tried to avoid over the last 20 years is not being completely crap.' U2 celebrated the artistic arc of their career, performing not only their classic songs 'Pride (In the Name of Love)' and 'I Still Haven't Found What I'm Looking For', but also their latest hit 'Vertigo' during the induction ceremony.

U2 also commemorated their breakthrough at Live Aid. Aligning with the 20th anniversary of the Live Aid concerts, the Live 8 concerts were a series of benefit concerts held from 2 to 6 July 2005 in cities including London, Philadelphia, Berlin and Moscow to raise awareness and funds for the Make Poverty History and the Global Call to Action Against Poverty campaigns. With performers including Coldplay, Dido, Madonna, Elton John, Pink Floyd and The Who, these campaigns were focused on eliminating poverty in developing countries and were held in advance of the G8 summit in Scotland to pressure world leaders to increase aid and forgive foreign debt. U2 performed 'Beautiful Day', 'Vertigo' and 'One', and joined Paul McCartney for a collaborative cover of The Beatles' 'Sgt. Pepper's Lonely Hearts Club Band'.

Though U2 were at a point where they could reflect on their history together, they continued to explore ways to innovate their sound. U2 began recording sessions for a new album at Abbey Road Studios during September 2006, bringing Rick Rubin on board to produce. However, it was soon apparent that U2 and Rubin had conflicting approaches to recording music and songwriting. Rubin wanted U2 to bring

finished and fully conceptualized songs into the studio, but this was not how U2 traditionally recorded together. The Edge told *Rolling Stone* that U2 did not finish any songs because 'it's in the process of recording that we really do our writing'. 'Rick strips everything away,' Adam told *Sun Media*. 'He doesn't like atmospherics and textures.' On these sessions, Rubin told *Q*, 'I don't know what their perspective was. I thought we had fun.'

Though they did not record an album together, two completed songs from the Rubin-produced sessions were released. The first was a 2006 collaboration with Green Day covering the 1979 song 'The Saints Are Coming' by the Scottish punk band Skids. Reinterpreting the lyrical imagery about drowning in a storm following the devastation of Hurricane Katrina the previous year in 2005, proceeds from the single benefitted Music Rising which was co-founded by the Edge to support music education and provide aid to musicians affected by natural disasters. U2 and Green Day performed 'The Saints Are Coming' during a football game at the Louisiana Superdome, the first game since being severely damaged by Hurricane Katrina. The other was 'Window In The Skies' which was released as a single in 2007 and was later nominated for a Grammy Award. Both songs would appear on U2's third greatest hits compilation *U218 Singles* released on 20 November 2006.

U2 resumed recording sessions in Fez, Morocco during May 2007, reuniting with Brian Eno and Daniel Lanois to produce the new album. For two weeks, U2 recorded at the hotel Riad El Yacout, turning its courtyard into a temporary studio. During the sessions, U2 attended the World Sacred Music Festival and became inspired by the music they were hearing, especially Persian vocalist Parisā. Other world-music performances, including Sufi singing and Joujouka drumming, were motivating U2 to be more experimental with the band-focused sound they had cultivated over the last few years. U2 recorded nearly a dozen songs while in Fez, with several songs recorded in a single take. The Edge, in *Hot Press*, called U2's sessions there a 'very fruitful experiment' which reminded him why he joined the band.

When U2 later resumed recording

Opposite top: Midge Ure, Sir Bob Geldof and Bono backstage at Live 8, Edinburgh, 2005. Opposite bottom: Bono sings with Billie Joe Armstrong of Green Day at the Superdome in New Orleans, Louisiana, 2006.

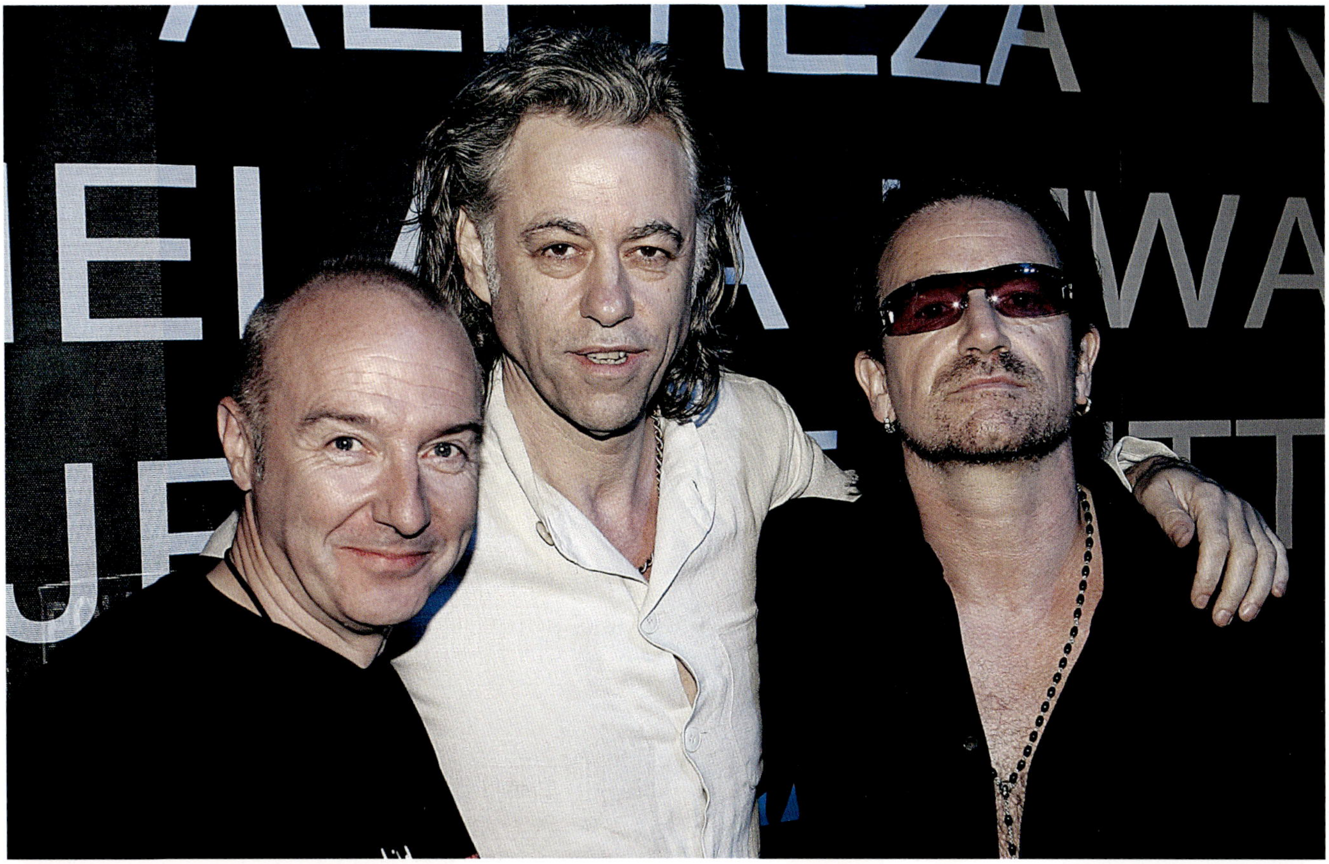

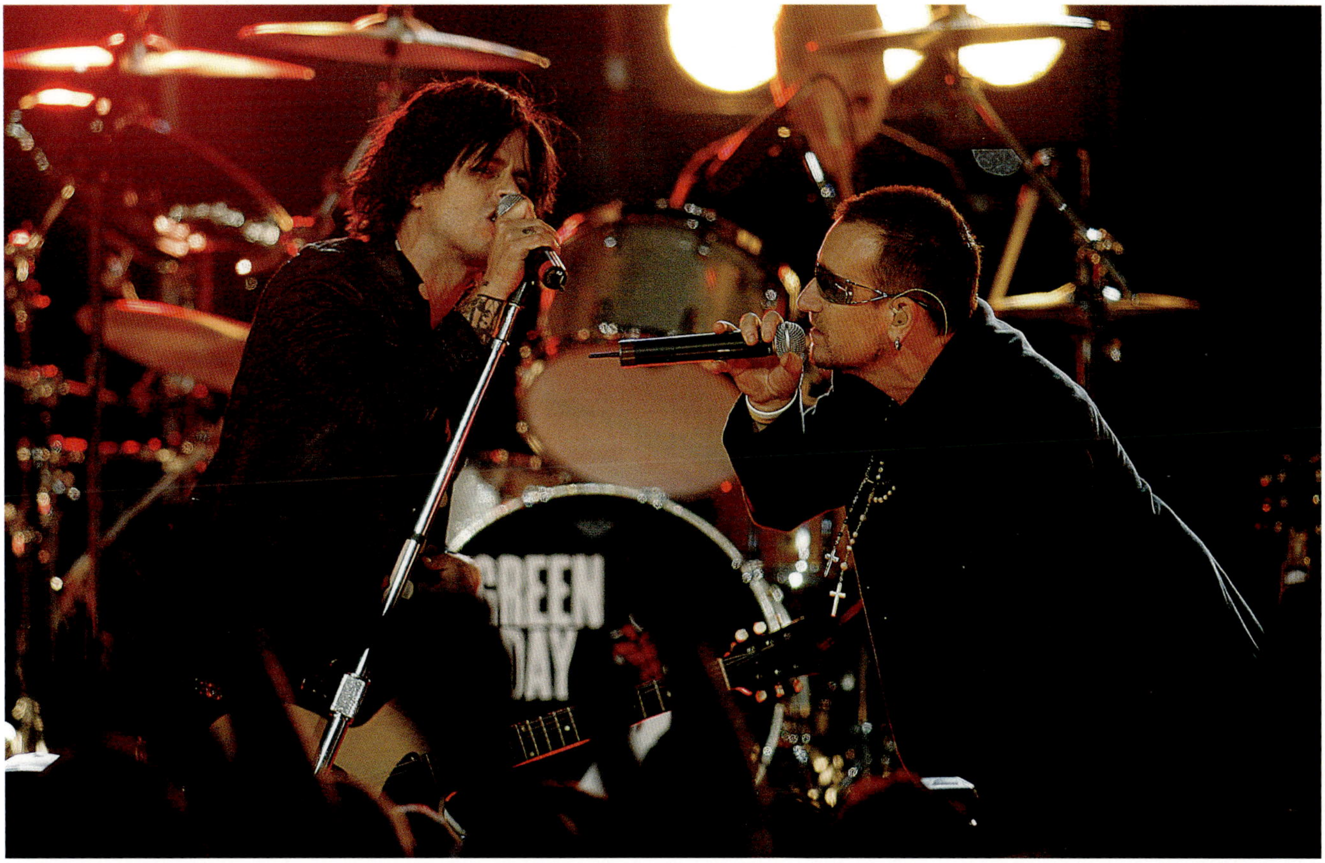

sessions at Hanover Quay Studios in Dublin, the excitement over the exoticism of the music they heard in Fez began to subside. Eno told *Pitchfork* in 2009 that most of the experimental world music was left out because it sounded synthetic and was not convincing enough, saying, 'We were very impressed by the music while we were there, but there was no realistic or emotionally satisfying way of marrying it using the music that we were doing, so in the end not very much of it at all showed through.' Bono agreed, telling the *Irish Independent*: 'We went so far out on the Sufi singing and the sort of ecstatic music front that we had to ground it and find a counterpoint'.

Though a lot of the musical elements from the Fez sessions were dropped, the songwriting concepts for the album were informed by some of the textural elements that remained, such as birds flying overhead, the band playing in the riad or people shopping at the local market. Leading up to the sessions, Bono felt that he was getting bored of writing songs in a first-person narrative. The exotic locales and sounds inspired him to write songs from different perspectives, using characters to tell a story or evoke a certain mood. 'It's a personal album,' Bono told *The Guardian* in 2009. 'These are very personal stories even though they are written in character and, in a way, couldn't be further from my own politics. But, in the sense of the peripheral vision, there's a world out there … You can feel it at the edges … But there is also a deliberate shutting out in order to focus on the more personal epiphanies.' Lanois told *National Post* in 2009 that Bono's vision for the songs was for them to become 'futuristic spirituals'.

In December 2008, U2 went to Olympic Studios in London to finish the album. Having composed over 50 songs during the sessions, the album was briefly delayed as U2 continued working to refine the songwriting and track listing. There were also discussions about releasing the songs across two EPs, *Daylight* and *Darkness*, but U2 ultimately decided to put out only one album. As most

of the song concepts for the album had originated while recording in Fez, these final sessions were spent picking which songs contributed to the spiritual narrative of the album.

U2 released *No Line on the Horizon* a couple of months later on 27 February 2009. The album received positive reviews upon release, with critics praising the band for musically challenging their more recent mainstream sound, but it did not earn the accolades and acclaim achieved by *All That You Can't Leave Behind* and *How to Dismantle an Atomic Bomb*. However, it was a commercial success, debuting on the charts at number one in 30 countries and becoming one of the top ten bestselling albums of the year.

'No Line On The Horizon', the album's titular opening song, was one of the earliest songs recorded for the album. It originated from several drum patterns that Larry was experimenting with that Eno then sampled for the Edge to improvise over. Using a fuzz pedal that Benjamin Curtis of the Secret Machines introduced him to, the Edge's playing made the song sound like 'space age rock 'n' roll'. The lyrics came to Bono after seeing photographs of Lake Constance by Japanese photographer Hiroshi Sugimoto titled *Boden Sea*.

'Magnificent', with lyrics inspired by Cole Porter and Bach, came out of a series of chord changes during a jam originally called 'French Disco' that the Edge said motivated everyone and described as inherently joyful and rare. It is also one of the songs that retained some of the world-music elements, featuring some Moroccan percussionists. It was released as a single with over a dozen remixes.

Developed after only a few hours, 'Moment of Surrender' was recorded in a single take. Eno told *The Guardian* in 2009 that recording the song was breathtaking and 'the most amazing studio experience I've ever had', adding that it was the song closest to the futuristic spiritual album concept. He strongly advocated for it to be released as the lead single. Bono described 'Moment of Surrender' as about a drug addict experiencing a crisis

Previous spread: U2, 2009.
Opposite: Bono, 2009

of faith. This theme continues on the next track, 'Unknown Caller', which was also recorded in a single take and is about the drug addict receiving mysteriously vague text messages on his mobile phone. Birdsong from the Fez sessions was added to the song's opening, creating a setting for the character in the song.

While initially developed in Fez, U2 found recording 'Stand Up Comedy' difficult and spent 6 months piecing it together, with the earliest version including Middle Eastern mandolins. Lanois said they spent so much time recreating 'Stand Up Comedy' that six different songs had formed. Bono said the lyrics were inspired by the 2008 anti-poverty campaign Stand Up and Take Action, and is about standing up to megalomaniac rock stars.

Two other singles were issued in addition to 'Magnificent', but came together after the Fez sessions. 'Get On Your Boots', the lead single, originated as a demo the Edge created using GarageBand which went through many changes. Bono wrote the lyrics about the time he saw planes flying out during the beginning of the Iraq War while on vacation in France with his family, relaying the experience in a narrative about a man writing a letter to his lover about what he had witnessed. The other single, 'I'll Go Crazy If I Don't Go Crazy Tonight', was a collaboration between U2 and will.i.am of the Black Eyed Peas who would also earn producer

credit. Partly inspired by Barack Obama's presidential election campaign, the song was recorded to give the album a brighter tone.

'Fez – Being Born' – originally slated to be the album opener before U2 felt a more energetic song was needed – came from two separate songs. 'Fez' was first developed during the Rubin sessions but later came into form when the Edge created an improvised symphonic guitar part. 'Being Born' was being worked on at the same time, and everyone felt each song complemented the other. 'I always look for outstanding transitional moments like that,' said Lanois. 'They can't be taken for granted. They have to be thought of scientifically.'

Closing out *No Line on the Horizon* are several character-driven songs that add depth to the album's concept. With a melody based on the hymn 'Veni, veni Emmanuel', 'White as Snow' was written from the viewpoint of a dying soldier in Afghanistan. U2 had been approached by Irish filmmaker Jim Sheridan to record an original song for his 2009 film *Brothers*. U2 then recorded 'White as Snow' and another song called 'Winter', with each having slightly different perspectives on the same story. 'Winter' was chosen for the film's soundtrack and earned U2 their fourth Golden Globe nomination for Best Original Song in 2010.

Developed by the Edge, 'Breathe' was nearly fully formed when Bono added stream-of-

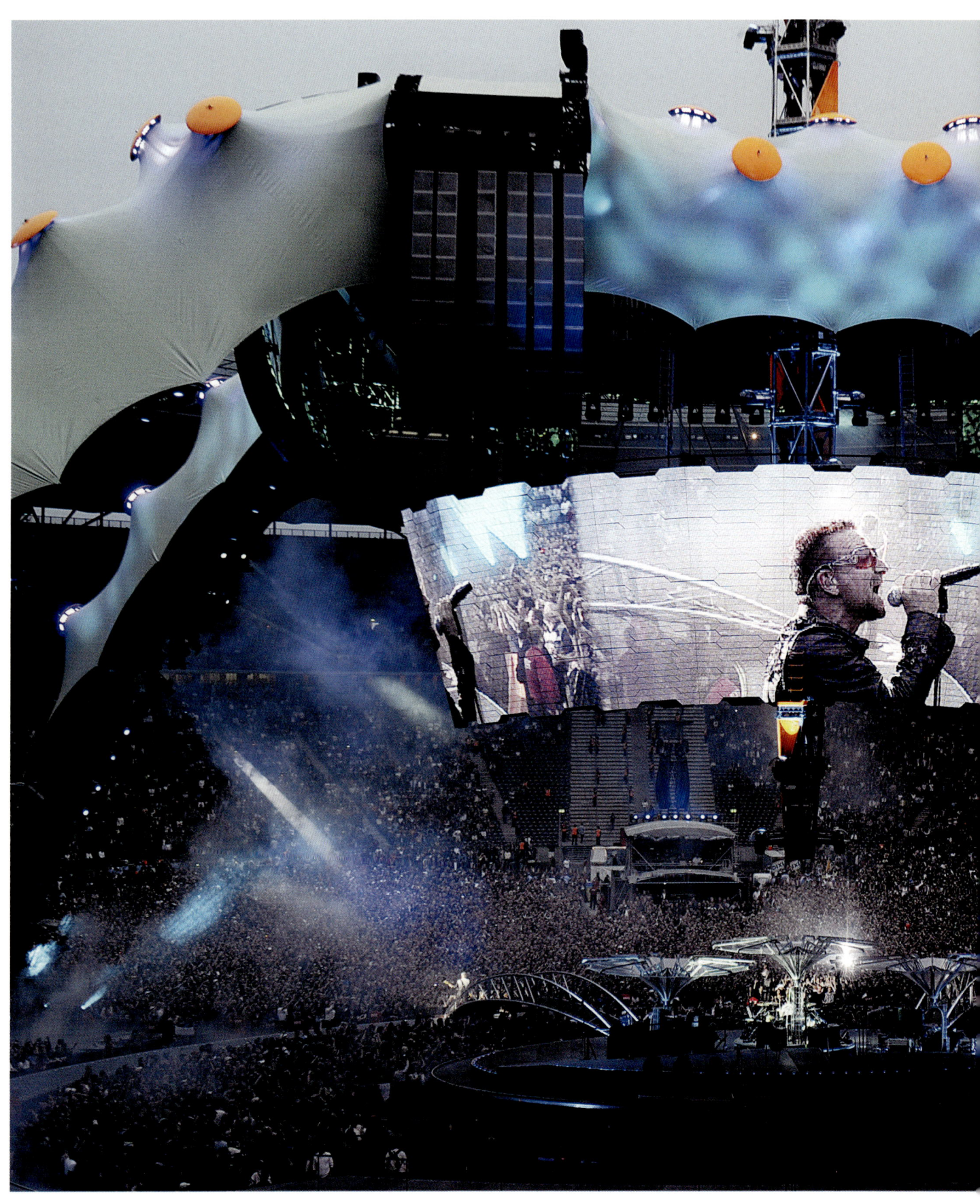

consciousness-style lyrics to it, having it take place on 16 June as a reference to Bloomsday from the James Joyce classic *Ulysses*. 'Breathe' was worked on extensively throughout recording *No Line on the Horizon*, with Bono going through different characters to drive the song's narrative and having him ultimately find redemption.

The final track on *No Line on the Horizon*, 'Cedars of Lebanon' is about a war correspondent documenting his experiences while reporting on a conflict. Bono sang the song from a first-person narrative, saying, 'I'd just kind of got worn out with my own biography.' For the music, Lanois took inspiration from *The Pearl*, a 1984 album collaboration between Eno and American composer Harold Budd.

These characters and their experiences from the album were then adapted into the plot of *Linear*, a 2009 film directed by Anton Corbijn which used songs from *No Line on the Horizon* and which was released as part of a deluxe version of the album. As opposed to being an extended music video, Corbijn described *Linear* as a new way to listen to a record by using film to create a connection with the music. Starring Saïd Taghmaoui, Lizzie Brocheré, Marta Barrio and Francisco Javier Malia Vazquez, *Linear* follows a Parisian motorcycle cop who leaves for Tripoli to see his girlfriend after becoming disillusioned by clashes between immigrants and police in the city.

To support *No Line on the Horizon*, U2 embarked on their U2 360° Tour in stadiums worldwide which became another technological marvel for its stage design. Further enhancing how to bridge a connection between U2 and the audience, the design featured a circular main stage in the centre that connected to an outer ring using movable rotating bridges, with the audience both inside and outside the outer ring. Stage designer Willie Williams described the design saying, 'The band is just sitting in the palm of the audience's hand.'

Towering above the stage was a four-legged structure affectionately referred to as 'The Claw', which at 164 feet is the largest stage ever constructed, and included at its centre a cylinder-shaped video screen that could expand and retract. The video screen projected graphics, videos and other effects, but it was also used to link up with the International Space Station and featured a recording of astronaut Mark Kelly holding up the words, 'It's a beautiful day' as well as another that featured astronauts singing lines from the Passengers' song, 'Your Blue Room'.

Running from June 2009 through July 2011, the U2 360° Tour included 110 shows across seven legs throughout five continents. By the end of it, it earned the record of highest-grossing tour ever at that time, with ticket sales exceeding $736 million. However, due to the costs of transporting the large stage, U2 barely turned a profit.

During the U2 360° Tour, U2 performed two concerts that highlighted other aspects of their legacy. On 11 November 2009, to commemorate the 20th anniversary of the fall of the Berlin Wall, U2 performed a short set at Brandenburg Gate in Berlin. A free event that was broadcast as part of MTV's Europe Music Awards, U2 performed 'Magnificent' and 'Moment Of Surrender' as well as some older songs, including Jay-Z guest rapping on 'Sunday Bloody Sunday'.

Two years later, U2 played a headlining show at the 2011 Glastonbury Festival for their first appearance there. They were originally scheduled to headline in 2010 but cancelled when Bono had back surgery. The setlist contained songs throughout their career, but featured more from *Achtung Baby* than any other album. During rehearsals for their Glastonbury gig, U2 filmed footage of them returning to Hansa Studios in Berlin to commemorate the album's 20th anniversary for the documentary *From the Sky Down*.

Both the festival concert and documentary capped a period that lasted longer than a decade in which U2 had looked back on their legacy while exploring new creative dynamics as a band. After playing together for over 30 years, they had a storied history that they could trace the path of their musical evolution through. They continued transforming themselves as artists, even while being celebrated for their contributions to music during the 1980s and 1990s, showing fans old and new alike that U2 never wanted to repeat themselves. U2 had spent the 2000s looking back on their own history as a band and how their music evolved, but now they were thinking about how far their lives had come since before there was even a band. By

the 2010s, with the landscape of the music industry so changed from when they started out, U2 were reaching back further to see the journey of innocence becoming experience.

Previous spread: The U2 360° Tour, Berlin, 2009.

5

Love Is All We Have Left

The new millennium saw U2 enter an era in which they could look back on their career while still defining it

. This was a period that began with U2 reclaiming their title as one of the biggest bands in the world, but that world would soon begin to look different. As new styles of music and ways to consume it emerged, reshaping the industry in seemingly real time, U2 now faced the challenge of understanding just exactly where they fitted in.

Disappointed by the comparatively lukewarm response to *No Line on the Horizon*, U2 had arrived at a creative crossroads. As rap and hip-hop began to gain cultural dominance and streaming and social media platforms had an impact on the music industry, the landscape of rock 'n' roll was changing. 'The commercial challenges have to be confronted,' said Adam. 'But I think, in a sense, the more interesting challenge is, "What is rock 'n' roll in this changing world?"'

In deciding how to follow their recent album, multiple projects were on the table. Bono publicly spoke about their next album being called *Songs of Ascent*, describing it to *The Observer* as a 'more meditative album on the theme of pilgrimage'. However, when U2 went into the studio to record the album, they were dissatisfied with the results.

Around this time, Bono and the Edge also had committed themselves to writing music and lyrics for the musical *Spider-Man: Turn Off the Dark*. When they were first pitched the project in 2002, it was appealing to Bono and the Edge because they had previously discussed producing something for Broadway, interested in the idea of creating an album that they would not have to tour themselves. Following the release of *No Line on the Horizon*, Bono told *Rolling Stone* that he wanted *Spider-Man* to be U2's next project. However, Larry and Adam were not interested in working on the musical, with Larry telling *Rolling Stone*, 'I'm feeling that it's the unfinished songs from [*No Line on the Horizon*] that we should be concentrating on.' Alluding to *Songs of Ascent*, Larry continued by saying, 'I think there's a part two of this record.' By the time it debuted to the public, *Spider-Man: Turn Off the Dark* had become the biggest flop in Broadway history, plagued by financial problems and production delays resulting from cast members injuring themselves during rehearsal and live performances.

Opposite: Actor Reeve Carney with Bono at a performance of *Spider-Man: Turn Off the Dark*

In addition to *Spider-Man* and *Songs of Ascent*, press reports also circulated about other potential U2 projects, including a traditional rock album produced by Danger Mouse and a dance album produced by RedOne and will.i.am. During October 2010, Bono claimed that U2 had finished recording 12 songs with Danger Mouse before realizing they were not going to complete the album before going on the final leg of the U2 360° Tour. Mixed messaging about the different albums continued until it was confirmed they were either shelved or cancelled altogether. In December 2011, Adam told *Q* that U2 initially thought they had enough songs left over from *No Line on the Horizon* to finish *Songs of Ascent*, but now they felt 'a long way from that material'. On the dance album, Adam told *Rolling Stone* that the recordings they did with RedOne were very exciting but that they did not feel like the right fit for U2, adding that he believed the Danger Mouse sessions came closest to capturing the essence of the band.

U2 continued recording with Danger Mouse throughout 2011 and 2012, with Bono telling RTÉ's *The Late Late Show* that they 'have to do something very special to have a reason to exist now.' By 2013, U2 went to Electric Lady Studios in New York to finish mixing the album, but were still not satisfied with the songs, with the Edge telling *Mojo* the songs were falling apart during mixing, saying, 'We'd allowed ourselves to think that "interesting" was enough.' After two years of recording, Danger Mouse stepped away from the album, with U2 then bringing in Ryan Tedder, Paul Epworth, Declan Gaffney and Flood to help complete it.

Though U2 did manage to release a song during this time, the band had a long-standing friendship with Nelson Mandela by the time they were approached in 2013 to contribute a song to the film based on his life, *Mandela: Long Walk to Freedom*. This chronicled his pursuit for equality during apartheid South Africa. U2 recorded 'Ordinary Love' while working on their new album, but Mandela had already been the subject of their music, with 'Breathe' for *No Line on the Horizon* being originally about him. 'Ordinary Love' was released during November 2013 and included the Mandela version of 'Breathe' as its B-side. It would go on to earn U2 their second Golden

Globe win as well as a second Academy Award nomination. When Mandela passed away during December 2013, U2 paused recording to mourn over their friend and hero.

Rumours of a new album continued, with *Billboard* reporting U2 would announce it with a commercial during Super Bowl XLVIII in February 2014. U2 would announce new music during the Super Bowl, but only a new digital single called 'Invisible' produced by Danger Mouse and released exclusively on Apple's iTunes Store as a partnership between (RED) and Bank of America. 'Invisible' was free to download for 36 hours, with Bank of America donating $1 to (RED) for every download, resulting in $3.1 million raised to fight the AIDS epidemic in Africa. Bono told *Rolling Stone* that 'Invisible' would not be on U2's new album, saying, 'We have another song we're excited about to kick off the album. This is just sort of a sneak preview – to remind people we exist.'

Recording continued throughout mid-2014, with Tedder, Epworth and Gaffney each involved at various stages to finish the album. Despite so many people involved, U2 welcomed the fresh perspectives they brought to the studio with them. 'We've always needed collaborators to challenge us,' Larry told *The Hollywood Reporter* in February 2014. 'We're slow learners. We need to be creative, on the cutting edge, challenged, and it's really hard going, it's relentless, and we're relentless, and we have a history of breaking engineers, producers. I mean, people come out of working with U2 and just go, '"I just don't know what's happened; it feels like a lifetime has passed by." And that's just the way we work.' By August 2014, however, continuing to delay their new album was no longer an option as another partnership deadline was fast approaching. As Gaffney worked with U2 during their final month in the studio, the Edge recalled in *Q* that most of the album had developed quickly towards the end of the sessions, with them sprinting to finish during the final four days of recording.

U2 finished recording their new album *Songs of Innocence* on 2 September 2014,

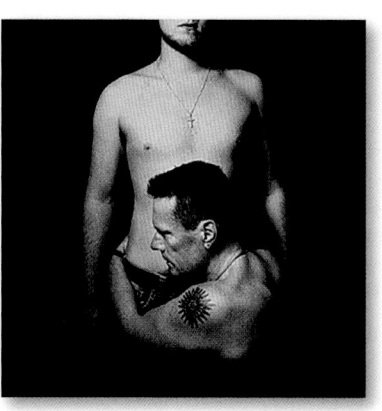

and when it was released one week later on 9 September, it was met with instant controversy. At the end of an Apple product launch event in Cupertino, California, U2 made a surprise appearance performing a new song called 'The Miracle (of Joey Ramone)'. After the performance, CEO Tim Cook announced with U2 that not only was their new album finished, but that it was being made immediately available for free to half a billion iTunes subscribers becoming what Cook called 'the largest album release of all time'. Bono called *Songs of Innocence* U2's most personal album yet, wanting to release it to 'as many people as possible, because that's what our band is all about.'

U2 were met with considerable backlash for releasing *Songs of Innocence* free to iTunes customers. Though they were reportedly paid a lump sum and Apple spent $100 million on marketing for Apple Music and the album, many musicians and industry experts criticized U2 for allegedly sending a message to consumers that suggested music should be free as opposed to being purchased as someone's art and livelihood.

There was also public outcry accusing Apple and U2 of adding music to people's libraries without permission, stemming from an opt-in feature in iTunes that automatically enabled music downloads. Critics agreed, lambasting U2 for prioritizing a corporation over their fans and other music consumers, and went as far as to describe *Songs of Innocence* as being nothing more than computer spam. To assist users who had automatic music downloads enabled, Apple released a website tool that allowed users to easily delete the album. Bono told *World Cafe* that U2 'wanted to deliver a pint of milk to people's front porches, but in a few cases it ended up in their fridge, on their cereal. People were like, "I'm dairy free."'

Paul McGuinness, who had retired as U2's manager in 2013, called the release a mistake, saying, 'People were unhappy about having something arrive that they hadn't asked for. It was easy enough to delete ... But I think that it should have been handled differently.' The

Apple CEO Tim Cook (L) announces the free download of the new U2 album on iTunes, California, 2014.

While *Songs of Innocence* is not a concept album in the strictest sense, the cohesiveness of the lyrical themes portrays a picture of a specific time and place. U2 do not necessarily find themselves stuck in the past, however, with the setting only serving as the backdrop for the various narratives that unfold throughout *Songs of Innocence*, with Bono saying, 'The whole album is first journeys – first journeys geographically, spiritually, sexually. And that's hard. But we went there.'

The band revisited the music of their youth as inspiration for *Songs of Innocence*. 'We listened to the music of that time (again) really to remind ourselves of the milieu, and what was the soundtrack of that particular moment in our lives, both personally and as the band,' said the Edge. 'We didn't set out to make an "homage" album, by any means.' This spirit is captured on the album's opening track, 'The Miracle (of Joey Ramone)', which pays tribute to the founding frontman of the Ramones, a band that had a big influence on U2 with Bono referring to them as 'the best punk rock band ever because they actually invented something.'

The Clash were another hugely influential

Previous spread: Bruce Springsteen and Adam Clayton perform for the World AIDS Day (RED) Concert at Times Square, New York, 2014.

Following spread: Aftermath of the Talbot Street bombings in Dublin, when three car bombs exploded simultaneously in the city. The Ulster Loyalist paramilitary group, the Ulster Volunteer Force (UVF), later claimed responsibility for the attacks.

group, and the song 'This Is Where You Can Reach Me Now' was inspired by them. It is dedicated to Joe Strummer, whom Bono describes in the liner notes as a soldier with a guitar as his weapon. 'We knew that we couldn't be as cool as The Clash', said Bono. 'That's proven to be true. But we did think we could get behind a sort of social justice agenda.' The song deals with Bono realizing that U2 had become his new family after his mother's death left a void in his childhood home.

'Volcano' also brings U2's punk influences to the fore and was written from the perspective of a teenage Bono giving his older self a hard time for how he has turned out. It was the last track finished for *Songs of Innocence* but was originally cut, as the band submitted a version to Apple that excluded the track before changing their minds as they felt the album was lopsided without it.

'California (There Is No End To Love)' chronicles U2's first time visiting America. 'I remember Edge, Adam, Larry and me getting off a plane in California,' recalled Bono, 'and looking at each other like, "this is better than the movies" and that was just the airport.'

Love is a theme that is woven throughout *Songs of Innocence*. Bono wrote 'Song for Someone' as a love song for his wife Ali, as they went on their first date the same month that Bono joined U2. He recalled in *Rolling Stone* how being young and in love clashed with the culture of Ireland at the time, describing the environment around him as hostile to 'the concept of the childhood sweetheart and a first love'. Originally meant for *No Line on the Horizon*, 'Every Breaking Wave' represents the difficulties of keeping that love alive as you surrender yourself to a partner.

Songs of Innocence also explores more complex aspects of love. 'Iris (Hold Me Close)' expresses how Bono still feels his mother's light and how that has shaped his journey as an artist. Its lyrics were inspired by a letter journalist James Foley wrote to his family before being killed by ISIS, with Bono writing the song about how we are all remembered by the simplest moments from our lives. The same month his mother passed, Bono met Ali but would not date her until a couple of years later, with him describing the song as 'dealing with some kind of transcendence of the female energy'. In *Surrender*, Bono said meeting Ali after his mother's death left him 'in the hands of another spirit guide'.

Other songs on *Songs of Innocence* reveal the violence that surrounded U2 during their childhood. 'Raised By Wolves' is about the aftermath of the 17 May 1974 bombings in Dublin and Monaghan carried out by the loyalist paramilitary group, the Ulster Volunteer Force, which killed 33 people. Bono and the Edge wrote the lyrics from the perspective of Andy Rowen, the brother of their friend Guggi, who witnessed the bombings and developed a heroin addiction to cope with the trauma.

'Cedarwood Road' is about the street Bono grew up on, telling Song Exploder he was often too afraid to leave his house. 'I grew up on Cedarwood Road,' said Bono in the album's liner notes. 'A nice street full of nice families. People who shaped my worldview. People I still admire and love … but there was a lot of violence in my teenage years … Cedarwood Road had some dark and hidden sides like all places.' However, Cedarwood Road also offered Bono a lifeline through his friend Guggi who was his neighbour, as the two found an escape from the violence through art. 'I think that we were a group of artists in the middle of a jungle who happened to be attracted to other people who weren't like everyone else,' remembers Guggi.

'It was disturbing to realize that my teenage life was largely dominated by memories of violence and my worldview was shaped by that,' said Bono.

'Sleep Like a Baby Tonight' is Bono remembering the institutional violence rampant throughout Ireland while growing up, from wives being beaten by their husbands to the priests who preyed upon young children. 'When the children of any church aren't served but are instead enslaved by an abuse of power,' said Bono, 'extraordinary acts of atonement are required to put things back together.'

Closing the album is 'The Troubles', a song Bono told Dave Fanning was 'an uncomfortable song about domestic violence'. The thematic dynamic of the song's narrative is elevated by guest vocals performed by Swedish singer Lykke Li, with Bono saying of Li, 'She puts us all under a spell with her music. We needed a feminine spirit; she was the right one.'

When U2 went on tour to support *Songs of Innocence*, they wanted to create a more intimate concert experience than they had with the U2 360° Tour. Going back to indoor arenas for the first time since the Vertigo Tour a decade earlier, the concept behind the Innocence + Experience Tour was to mirror the journey on the album, with U2 metaphorically passing from 'innocence' to 'experience'. On how this theme developed for the tour, stage designer Willie Williams told *Live Design* in 2015 'Every U2 tour has had some kind of touchstone from which everything has grown – white flags, The Blues, architecture, a job reapplication, and of course, once it all stemmed from a pair of wrap-around shades. On this project, the genesis was narrative. It's the narrative that runs through the album: the story of four teenagers growing up in '70s Dublin looking out of their bedroom windows and trying to figure out how they fit into the often violent and disrupted world outside.'

This creative direction would influence the tour's stage design. The main stage, with floor illuminations in the shape of an 'I' to represent 'innocence', connected to the B-stage, with an illuminated 'E' for 'experience', via a long walkway that bisected the venue and which symbolized the band's musical journey between the two. Suspended parallel above the walkway was a semi-transparent, double-sided video cage that could simultaneously display video graphics and, supported by a catwalk inside the cage, allow the band to perform juxtaposed with the visuals. While performing 'Cedarwood Road', Bono paced along the video cage's internal catwalk with the video graphics projecting the street he grew up on, creating the effect of him strolling through a caricature of his old neighbourhood.

While *Songs of Innocence* was not appreciated by many largely due to the way it was released, the Innocence + Experience Tour was praised for how U2 utilized the production to elevate the themes and narratives of the album, with some critics even suggesting that *Songs of Innocence* now warranted a reassessment because of the tour. Philip Cosores, in his review of their concert in Los Angeles for *Consequence of Sound*, said U2's live rendition of these songs 'even argued that perhaps the most recent U2 output was given an unfair shake from critics more interested in attacking the new album's release method than the actual songs'. U2 took the Innocence

+ Experience Tour to North America and Europe, playing 76 shows from May through December 2015.

The final night would become the tour's most memorable, though. U2 were originally scheduled to play four concerts in Paris from 10 to 15 November, but cancelled the final two following the series of terrorist attacks carried out across the city on 13 November, one of which included a mass shooting during an Eagles of Death Metal concert at the Bataclan theatre where 89 people were murdered. The two concerts were postponed until 6 and 7 December, making them the new final nights of the tour. When U2 returned to Paris for the first concert, with the weight of the tragedy on his mind, Bono told the audience, 'Tonight we are all Parisian. If you love liberty, then Paris is your home town.' Patti Smith later joined U2 onstage to close out the encore, performing 'Bad' as well as her unifying anthem, 'People Have the Power'. During the second night's encore, at the end of the tour, U2 invited Eagles of Death Metal onstage with them to perform Patti Smith's 'People Have the Power', their first time back onstage since the Bataclan attack. After the performance, U2 gave their stage and instruments over to Eagles of Death Metal, leaving them to perform their song 'I Love You All the Time', a gesture Bono recalls in *Surrender* was done 'so that rock 'n' roll, in their voice, not ours, would have its say'.

On the same day *Songs of Innocence* was released on iTunes, Bono had announced U2's next album in a post on the band's website, saying, 'If you like *Songs of Innocence*, stay with us for *Songs of Experience*. It should be ready soon enough … although I know I've said that before …' As it would turn out, *Songs of Experience* would not be ready soon.

After putting out *Songs of Innocence*, the Edge told *Rolling Stone* U2 had enough material to release two separate albums, saying, 'The majority of the unfinished songs are worthy of becoming part of *Songs of Experience* and some are already as good or better than anything on *Songs of Innocence*.' He also added that while he hoped this album would not take as long to record, U2 would only release it when it was ready.

However, recording for *Songs of Experience* was delayed when Bono, during November 2014, suffered serious injuries related to a bicycle crash in Central Park. In a post on the band's website published on New Year's Day 2015, Bono provided an update on his condition, saying he now had a titanium elbow and that he was unsure if he could ever play guitar again. While healing from his injuries, Bono took time to improve the album's songwriting, telling *Q*, 'The gift of it was that I had time to write while in the mentality that you get to at the end of an album.' The Edge echoed Bono's perspective in *The New York Times*, pointing out that a band was at the height of their creative power towards the end of an album, saying, 'Bono is trying to capitalize on that momentum and that sharpness'. With this new clarity, U2 would continue to refine the songs for *Songs of Experience*.

When recording for *Songs of Experience* began in early 2015, British musician Andy Barlow of the electronic music duo Lamb was brought in to produce, working with U2 for two weeks in Monaco and then an additional six weeks during April and May while the band began tour rehearsals in Vancouver. With the help of a mobile recording studio, U2 continued working on the album during impromptu sessions between concerts, which Barlow said broke with the tradition of how U2 typically worked. 'They've never really done anything like this before,' he told *Billboard*, adding that Bono usually liked to work on an album after U2 finished touring.

Reports circulated that *Songs of Experience* would be released soon but delays continued. In October 2015, Bono told *Entertainment Weekly* that U2 had completed 18 songs, whereas the Edge told *Hot Press* they hoped to release the album by the end of 2016. After the Innocence + Experience Tour ended in Paris during December 2015, U2 continued working on *Songs of Experience* during early 2016 at Rick Rubin's recording studio

Previous spread, left: The Experience Innocence Tour at The Forum in Los Angeles, 2018. Opposite: U2 pay their respects and place flowers on the pavement near the scene of the Bataclan Theatre terrorist attack in Paris, November 2016.

Shangri-La in Los Angeles. In March 2016, they relocated to a Victorian mansion outside Dublin, working with British music producer Jolyon Thomas and turning the parlour into a provisional studio, with Ryan Tedder later joining the sessions in May. 'We are trying to really be brutal with the material and only focus on the things we're really convinced are the best ideas …' the Edge told *Rolling Stone*. 'Things are still in their rough state, but sounding really great.'

U2 were set to release *Songs of Experience* by the end of 2016, but two major world events forced them to reconsider the songs and to revisit the album. The first was the Brexit referendum during June 2016 in which the United Kingdom became the first and only country to leave the European Union, of which it had been a member since 1973.

The other was Donald Trump winning the 2016 United States presidential election over former Secretary of State and First Lady Hillary Clinton. As this new wave of populist conservatism affected the dynamic of global politics, U2 wanted to revisit the tone of *Songs of Experience* which delayed its release even further. In April 2017, Bono told *Mojo* that the album would not become political overnight. The Edge recalled in September 2017 that U2 were reassessing 'if the album we had just finished was what we wanted to say'. In a video previously posted on their website on Christmas Day 2016, U2 had said that *Songs of Experience* would be released in 2017, but these recent interviews were proving that to be increasingly unlikely.

Recording had been delayed again when, in 2016 between Christmas and New Year's Day, Bono was admitted to the hospital for emergency open-heart surgery. In *Surrender*, Bono revealed that the operation was for a blister that formed in his aorta due to him having a bicuspid aortic valve. It was a near-death experience for Bono, one that further influenced his songwriting by adding feelings of mortality that expanded the tone and narrative of the album. Recalling feeling especially creatively inspired to revisit *Songs of Experience* with this new perspective, not dissimilar to how he felt leading up to the recording of *All That You Can't Leave Behind*, Bono told *Rolling Stone* in December 2017 that 'not surrendering to melancholy is the most important thing if you are going to fight

Opposite: U2 play the O2 Arena in London, 2018.

your way out of whatever corner you are in'. Following Bono's recovery, U2 returned to Electric Lady Studios in March 2017, working with Steve Lillywhite to rerecord songs. Adam told *Mojo* in March that U2 had completed 16 songs that would be narrowed down to a final dozen, with the Edge confirming in September 2017 that U2 had compiled a final track listing but that some songs were still undergoing lyrical changes. Barlow told *Billboard* that Bono was making changes to the lyrics even while the album was being mastered.

During the middle of recording *Songs of Experience*, U2 embarked on a whole new tour to celebrate the 30th anniversary of *The Joshua Tree*. Originally planned as a single show in both the United States and Europe, U2 expanded the concept to a proper full tour, taking the Joshua Tree Tour 2017 across North America, Europe and South America from May through October 2017. Just as the 2016 presidential election affected the tone of Songs of Experience, so did it motivate U2 to reassess one of their most beloved albums. The Edge told *Rolling Stone*, regarding the ongoing relevance of the themes of *The Joshua Tree*, 'Things have kind of come full circle, if you want. That record was written in the mid-1980s, during the Reagan–Thatcher era of US and UK politics. It was a period when there was a lot of unrest … It feels like we're right back there in a way. I don't think any of our work has ever come full circle to that extent.'

While U2's tours since the early 1990s had been technical marvels, the original design for the Joshua Tree Tour was anything but, with its emphasis on minimalism. Using a design philosophy stage designer Willie Williams calls 'maximal minimalism', the Joshua Tree Tour 2017 featured a 200-foot wide 7.6K resolution screen that became the largest and highest resolution screen in concert history, with a silhouette of a Joshua tree imposed on the screen and a B-stage that extended from the main stage as its shadow.

For the Joshua Tree Tour 2017, U2 performed the entirety of *The Joshua Tree* for the first time and in album sequence. There were initial concerns about how that approach would go over in a concert setting, as 'Where the Streets Have No Name' had become a staple of U2's encores, but as an album opener, the flow of the concert would change. 'People react a little differently when they know what's coming next,' said Adam in *Mojo*, 'and they also react a little differently when they're having an internal relationship with that particular running order.' To address this, U2 designed the show in three acts: the first focusing on the band's earlier songs, the second featuring *The Joshua Tree* and the third including more recent songs. The screen also depicted short videos by Anton Corbijn, which included visuals that reflected the images and themes of *The Joshua Tree* and the concert's other songs.

The Joshua Tree Tour 2017 also saw the introduction of a new character by Bono, the first since Zoo TV. For his performance of 'Exit' that followed a clip from the 1950s western television programme *Trackdown* – which featured a man named Trump swindling a town by promising its citizens he would build a wall to protect them – Bono stepped into the role of the Shadow Man, a demented preacher loosely modelled after the character Hazel Motes from Flannery O'Connor's novel *Wise Blood*. The Joshua Tree Tour 2017 also saw the first live performance of 'Red Hill Mining Town', the only song from the album never played live during the original tour.

Contributing to the tour's political themes, the final act featured songs that paid tribute to women, with Williams telling *U2.com*, 'The thought was that we are currently living in a time when we could really use a more feminine spirit in our leadership and a way to illustrate this might be to celebrate some of the great female pioneers of the past.' The Joshua Tree Tour 2017 earned critical praise for its performances and production, surprising many who thought the tour meant U2 had become a legacy act riding on the coat-tails of nostalgia. The tour won several awards for its production and design.

A little over a month after the tour ended, U2 finally released *Songs of Experience* on 1 December 2017. While *Songs of Innocence* focused on U2 growing up in Ireland, its companion represented letters from Bono addressed to the people closest to him, the album pairing drawing inspiration from William Blake's 1794 anthology of poems *Songs of Innocence and of Experience*. The album debuted at number one in several countries, making U2 the first band to earn number one albums in every decade since the 1980s, and also earned more positive reviews than its predecessor.

Opposite: Adam Clayton performs during the World Stage event as part of the MTV EMAs in London, 2017.
Next spread: The Joshua Tree Tour, 2017.

The album opening centres on Bono's brush with mortality in 'Love Is All We Have Left', a song he told *Rolling Stone* has his favourite opening line on a U2 album. It thematically bridges a connection to their previous album, with Bono adding, 'In the second verse, innocence admonishes experience.' The next track, 'Lights of Home', which features HAIM, continues with the theme of mortality as Bono declares in the song's opening that he should not even be alive now. He told *The Sunday Times* that 'Lights of Home' was written because he had felt such fear over his near-death experience that it led to a new-found appreciation for wanting to stay alive, doing things like spending more time with his wife and kids. 'When I admitted I was afraid,' Bono said, 'my faith returned.'

Several songs on the album are letters addressed to his wife Ali. Released as the first single, and inspired by Motown, Bono wrote 'You're The Best Thing About Me' after having a nightmare about his marriage falling apart, referring to the song as a portrait of an idiot going through a midlife crisis. U2 worked so closely to the deadline that they even rerecorded the song a week before releasing it as a single. 'Landlady' was also written for Ali, remembering a time when she worked for an insurance company to pay the bills while Bono was getting U2 off the ground. It is a tribute in which Bono sings she kept him from being a starving artist.

'The Showman (Little More Better)' is a love letter to U2's audience. Bono describes the song as being about not trusting performers too much, but also says that he appreciates that U2's fans have trusted them for all these years, further shaping them and their relationship to their own music. 'We give birth to these songs,' says Bono, 'but it is our audience who give life and meaning to them.'

A song that Bono says is where 'innocence challenges experience', 'The Little Things That Give You Away' is a letter to his younger self. Bono says that by the end of the song, after having been dressed down for the type of person he grew up to be, 'experience breaks down' and he 'admits his deepest fears'. It is the first song from *Songs of Experience* that U2 debuted, playing it live as the closing song during their opening night concert of the Joshua Tree Tour 2017 in Vancouver.

'Get Out Of Your Own Way' bridges the album's letter concept with its more political themes, the ideas that resulted in its delayed release a result of the songs being reworked to reflect current global issues. Written as a letter from Bono to his daughters about not becoming your own worst enemy, it also evokes imagery surrounding the political crisis in the United States. The song features vocals from rapper Kendrick Lamar, playing a character Bono refers to as a 'cracked preacher'. 'There's a righteous anger that is hard to argue with,' said Bono of Lamar. 'I asked him would he rap about where America is at; his reply was to rap about where America isn't.'

Lamar's vocal then segues into 'American Soul', which addresses the worsening of the existential threat facing America. U2 reworked *Songs of Experience* because, according to the Edge, 'to ignore what was happening in America would be just weird', calling Trump's leadership style as 'fear politics of the most cynical type'. The Edge also added, 'I think we share a lot of values with Kendrick'. Prior to the release of *Songs of Experience*, Lamar sampled the song for the track 'XXX' from his Pulitzer Prize-winning 2017 album *DAMN*.

'Summer of Love', featuring Lady Gaga on backing vocals, reappropriates the 1967 hippy culture slogan to address the human rights abuses that Syrian president Bashar al-Assad carried out against his own citizens in Aleppo during November and December 2016. The Edge said the song's core idea came from a news story about a gardener in Aleppo who defiantly grew flowers as a political statement. The war in Syria also makes its way into 'Red Flag Day', notably the refugee crisis in which millions of people were displaced and forced to find sanctuary or asylum migrating to Europe and elsewhere. The Edge said that looking out at the Mediterranean Sea, the same one in which people were fighting for their lives to cross on makeshift rafts, really put things into perspective and shaped the tone of the album.

'The Blackout' is the most sonically aggressive political song on *Songs of Experience*. The lyrics evoking extinction have dual meanings, one about the diminishing appeal of an ageing rock star and the other about the crumbling of democracy. 'It's a letter to the moment we're in,' said Bono, 'where both the personal and political apocalypse combine.'

Following spread:
The Edge, Matthew McConaughey and Bono at the premiere of *Sing 2* at the Greek Theatre in Los Angeles, 2021.

'Love Is Bigger Than Anything In Its Way' contains the album's most optimistic political statement, with Bono telling *iHeartRadio* that the song was about overcoming hardships with love and that he came up with the title following the November 2015 attacks in Paris. The music video for 'Love Is Bigger Than Anything In Its Way' celebrated Dublin's inclusive and diverse communities, becoming an LGBTQ+ and allyship anthem, and was introduced by a young woman saying, 'You don't care about what other people think any more. It's about kind of what you feel about yourself and what you kind of want to bring to the world.'

Closing out *Songs of Experience* is '13 (There Is A Light)', which references 'Song For Someone' from *Songs of Innocence*, and is about progressing from nothing towards what brings light into our lives. 'There are a lot of songs about light in the U2 repertoire,' said Adam. 'It's an image of faith and obviously people having near-death experiences describe seeing a bright light.' Praising kindness and the value of innocence as the way to keep one's inner light shining bright, it is a captivating way to close the journey from innocence to experience.

U2 took *Songs of Experience* out on the road in May 2018 for the Experience + Innocence Tour, reprising the concept and stage design from its previous companion tour. While technical enhancements were made to the stage design, including a higher resolution screen and LED panels added to the 'experience' B-stage floor, thematic changes were made to the setlist, visual graphics and narrative. While Bono would walk onstage performing the vocal opening of 'The Miracle (of Joey Ramone)' at the beginning of shows for the Innocence + Experience Tour, concerts on the Experience + Innocence Tour would begin with X-ray visuals signifying Bono's mortality and him performing 'Love Is All We Have Left' from the cage above the stage walkway.

The political themes from the album were also heightened on this tour, including visuals projecting messages such as 'Refugees welcome', 'Vote' and 'None of us are equal until all of us are equal' during the pre-show. During the European leg of the tour, U2 played clips of Charlie Chaplin delivering his famous anti-fascist monologue from his 1941 film *The Great Dictator*. The tour also saw the return of MacPhisto from Zoo TV, appearing more devilishly sinister 25 years since his first appearance, telling audiences that he does his best work to spread confusion

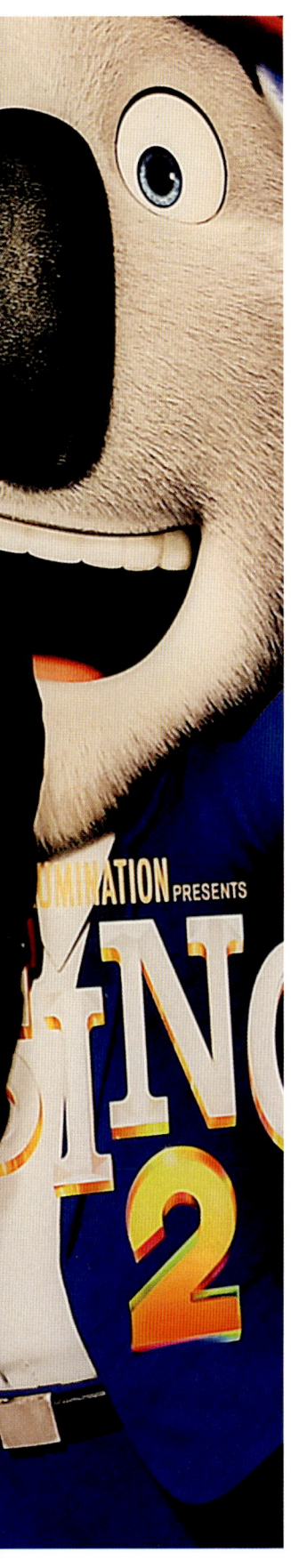

when autocrats like Vladimir Putin and Viktor Orbán obfuscate truth. While Bono performed in costume as MacPhisto for Zoo TV, the character's return for the Experience + Innocence Tour was instead manifested using augmented reality, using a tablet device to create a filter effect on Bono's face that is visible on the screens.

During the intermission, a comic-book-style animation played, depicting U2's musical evolution, set to St. Francis Hotel's 'Gotham Experience Remix' version of 'Hold Me, Thrill Me, Kiss Me, Kill Me' which included vocal performances from Gavin Friday and Arcade Fire's Régine Chassagne. For the concert finale, just like with *Songs of Experience*, '13 (There Is a Light)' closed the show as Bono revealed a light bulb emerging from a miniature replica of his childhood home. The Experience + Innocence Tour ran through November 2018 and included 60 shows across two legs in North America and Europe.

During the tour, U2 also played a one-off show in June 2018 at the historic Apollo Theatre in Harlem. A vastly more intimate performance than they were accustomed to, U2 played to 1,500 people and were accompanied by the 13-piece Sun Ra Arkestra for the encore, with the entire concert airing on Sirius XM. That month, a U2-themed radio station called 'The U2 Experience' premiered on Sirius XM for a limited time. Two years later, in July 2020, U2's partnership with Sirius XM would expand into a permanent station called U2-X Radio.

During November and December 2019, U2 took *The Joshua Tree* back out on the road again for the Joshua Tree Tour 2019. The tour marked U2's return to Australia and New Zealand for the first time since the U2 360° Tour, and also saw them making their live debut in several Asian countries including South Korea, Singapore, the Philippines and India. To celebrate their first concert in India, U2 collaborated with musician A. R. Rahman for a new single called 'Ahimsa'.

U2 were also embracing technology to reach fans in new ways. On St Patrick's Day in 2020, during the onset of the Covid-19 pandemic, Bono performed a new song on Instagram. A piano ballad called 'Let Your Love Be Known', it was written to honour the people of Italy affected by the coronavirus. Bono was inspired by their singing to each

other from balconies and rooftops. 'For the Italians who inspired it … for the Irish … for ANYONE who this St. Patrick's Day is in a tight spot and still singing,' the Instagram post said. 'For the doctors, nurses, carers on the front line, it's you we're singing to.'

In celebration of his 60th birthday in May 2020, Bono released a playlist on streaming platforms called '60 Songs That Saved My Life', meaning, 'The ones I couldn't have lived without … the ones that got me from there to here, zero to 60 … through all the scrapes, all manner of nuisance, from the serious to the silly … and the joy, mostly joy.' The playlist included beloved songs from Bono's childhood as well as more recent songs and collaborations. Each song was accompanied by an open letter Bono wrote to that artist, with each expressing his gratitude and fascination with them. 'I wanted to thank the artists and everyone who helped make them,' said Bono. 'They were doing the same for me.'

U2 relaunched their official YouTube channel in September 2020, remastering all their music videos in 4K HD, as well as highlighting never-before-seen footage and live performances. During March 2021, U2 unveiled *U2: The Virtual Road*, a limited release streaming series consisting of four concert videos rereleased with remastered audio. As the concert industry was still impacted by Covid-19, *U2: The Virtual Road* became a way for U2 to connect with audiences through some of their most iconic performances, including *U2: Live At Red Rocks* from 1983, *PopMart: Live From Mexico City* from 1997, *U2 Go Home: Live from Slane Castle* from 2001 and *Innocence + Experience: Live in Paris* from 2015. 'Every show is memorable for us but these four particularly so … It's exciting to be on the road again … Embracing all the wonder of the virtual road,' said U2 on their website.

U2 also made their debut on TikTok in November 2021, premiering a clip from their new song, 'Your Song Saved My Life'. The song was U2's contribution to the soundtrack for the animated musical film *Sing 2*, which also co-starred Bono as Clay Calloway, a reclusive lion who is also the world's most famous rock star.

U2 also continued to use their platform to champion their political convictions. Russia's invasion of Ukraine in February 2022 became

the largest attack in Europe since World War II, resulting in much of the world rallying their support for Ukraine and its sovereignty. Along with other artists like Bruce Springsteen, Sting, Kacey Musgraves and Carole King, Bono and the Edge participated in the Stand Up for Ukraine livestream organized by Global Citizen, an international advocacy organization dedicated to promoting social justice and equity. The duo performed an alternative version of 'Walk On', updating its lyrics to reflect the people of Ukraine fighting for their freedom. The following month, in March 2022, at the invitation of Ukraine's president Volodymyr Zelenskyy, Bono and the Edge travelled to the war's front line, playing an impromptu concert in a Kyiv subway station. In front of a crowd of 100 Ukrainian civilians and soldiers, they performed a 40-minute set that included acoustic versions of U2's hits like 'With Or Without You', 'Desire' and 'Angel of Harlem'. They were also joined by Ukrainian singer Taras Topolia, as well as members of his band Antytila, to perform a version of Ben E. King's 1961 classic 'Stand by Me', updating its lyrics to become 'Stand by Ukraine'. 'The people in Ukraine are not just fighting for your own freedom, you are fighting for all of us who love freedom,' Bono said to the crowd. 'We pray that you will enjoy some of that peace soon.'

During November 2022, Bono released his memoir *Surrender: 40 Songs, One Story*, which chronicled his life and career. The same month, he embarked on a 14-city book tour in small theatres across the United States and Europe. 'I miss being onstage and the closeness of U2's audience,' Bono said. 'In these shows, I've got some stories to sing, and some songs to tell ...' Dubbed the Stories of Surrender Tour, Bono shared stories and acted out scenes from his book, accompanied by stripped-down versions of U2's greatest songs performed by Jacknife Lee on keyboards and percussion, Kate Ellis on cello and Gemma Doherty on harp. The tour was later extended to include a residency at the Beacon Theatre in New York during April and May 2023.

U2 also had the chance to witness the impact of their legacy when they received the Kennedy Center Honors during December 2022, an award given out by the John F. Kennedy Center for the Performing Arts to celebrate performers who made significant contributions to the enrichment of American culture. Joined by other influential entertainers such as George Clooney, Gladys Knight and Amy Grant, who each received recognition for their cultural impact, U2 were recognized for their nearly 50 years together as an 'intact and, more compellingly, an active, creative unit'. Actors Sean Penn and Sacha Baron Cohen, the latter performing as his character Borat, each paid tribute to U2, with Penn calling U2 'one of the most poignant and consistently relevant bands in history', and adding that 'Bono has often said that being famous is nonsense, celebrity is nonsense, but it is currency. And the band has spent its currency to show the usefulness of art in the world.' A video tribute was also shared, featuring clips of other musicians like Beyoncé, Harry Styles and Billie Eilish all reciting U2 lyrics. The tribute closed with Pearl Jam frontman Eddie Vedder performing 'Elevation' and 'One', while Brandi Carlile, Hozier and Ukrainian singer Jamala united for a rendition of 'Walk On'.

As all this was happening, U2 were quietly working on a new musical project. With the pandemic lockdowns implemented around the world, U2 found themselves with more free time as most people were largely confined to their homes. This allowed Bono to finish his memoir and revisit an earlier project in which U2 would rerecord their songs as a way to understand them more in relation to their long career and evolving musical style. The idea for the album, as the Edge told *The Telegraph*'s Neil McCormick, was to see if their songs worked well with a more intimate arrangement and performed 'as if Bono was singing in your ear'. Considering the isolation that came with life during the pandemic, they opted for a softer approach over their usual anthemic bombast by focusing on the core emotions and themes of their music. With both the memoir and rerecording projects happening at the same time, one began to influence the other's development. Bono based each of the 40 chapters of his book on different U2 songs and the Edge advocated that U2 rerecord the 40 songs from those chapters. Adam told *Billboard* that the Edge said he would 'come up with a different space for those songs so we can present them in a way where the narrative of the song in some way is associated to the arc of the book'.

Previous spread: U2 pose with their awards following the Artists Dinner at the US Department of State in Washington, DC, 2022. Opposite: Bono's biography, Surrender. Following spread: Bono and Stephen Spielberg at the Berlin Film Festival, 2023.

Sessions for the rerecording album began during early 2021 and continued over a two-year period, with the Edge taking the lead on developing the basic structure of each song. In order to understand the core of the song and how it could transcend the original version, as well as not giving in to the cheap allure of nostalgia, the Edge was not precious about the source recording, saying, 'We gave ourselves permission to disregard any sense of reverence for the originals. What I learnt was that the best songs are kind of indestructible.' The Edge would change a song's original key, rhythm or chords, and then build ideas around them using acoustic guitar and piano to create a more intimate musical aesthetic. The way the Edge approached this process was also meant to complement Bono's vocals, lowering keys to accommodate Bono's current vocal range, a necessary decision as much of U2's earlier work was meant to be played live when Bono used to sing at a much higher register. 'You serve the song by serving the singer,' the Edge said. 'Bono's voice has a deeper resonance, he has access to tones he never had before. He has also lost any self-consciousness. He still has the big notes, but we've learnt to use them less often. He knows better how to use his voice as an interpretive tool, which comes with experience.'

With the Edge focused on breaking each song down to its most essential arrangement, there was not much need for Adam and Larry to contribute a rhythm section to many of the songs. This ultimately made the album a U2 project driven by Bono and the Edge. However, while the album's rhythm sections were more subdued, Adam and Larry still performed on some tracks. Coincidentally, during the recording process, Larry required back surgery and did not feel well enough to perform with a full drum kit. While he did play some percussion during the sessions, they largely used drum loops he had previously recorded. Adam told *Mojo* that he was not sure whether his bass contributions would be used in the final mixes, but had understood the album as being similar to those by Simon & Garfunkel, meaning 'essentially acoustic guitar tracks that there were some rhythmic elements added to'.

U2's collection of stripped-down reinterpretations of their earlier songs would be released on 17 March 2023 as *Songs of Surrender*. In January 2023, the Edge mailed out 40 photocopies of a handwritten letter to select U2 fans around the world, teasing the forthcoming release of *Songs of Surrender*. The album was officially announced the same month when U2 uploaded a video to social media featuring a rerecorded version of 'Beautiful Day'. The first single released for *Songs of Surrender* was 'Pride (In the Name of Love)', followed by new versions of 'With Or Without You', 'One', 'Beautiful Day' and 'Invisible' in the lead-up to the album's release. While many songs received alternative arrangements with minor lyrical or structural changes, others had evolved a lot from their original, such as the new version of 'Where the Streets Have No Name' forgoing its signature guitar opening for a cello performed by HAUSER. 'Walk On' received significant lyrical changes, now retitled as 'Walk On (Ukraine)' in support of Volodymyr Zelenskyy and his opposition to Russia invading Ukraine.

Nearly 50 songs were rerecorded during the sessions. While U2's intention was to have the track listing of *Songs of Surrender* reflect the chapter titles in *Surrender*, the two projects only shared 28 songs out of the potential 40. Snippets of the rerecorded songs included for *Songs of Surrender*, as well as those not chosen for it, were included as introductions to each chapter of the audiobook version of *Surrender*. U2 covered songs from every album in their career apart from *October* and *No Line on the Horizon* as well as the Passengers' project *Original Soundtracks 1*.

To coincide with their new album, Bono and the Edge released a streaming special the same day as *Songs of Surrender*. *Bono & the Edge: A Sort of Homecoming*, released exclusively on Disney+, featured the duo taking David Letterman around Dublin during the American talk-show legend's first visit to Ireland. The documentary also covered U2's journey as a band after 45 years together, featuring interviews as well as performances by Bono and the Edge at the Ambassador Theatre. *A Sort of Homecoming* also included a new song called 'Forty Foot Man', a song Bono and the Edge wrote for Letterman in the middle of the night after they took a trip to the Forty Foot, a chilly bathing pool along the Dublin Bay. 'Many nice things have happened to me for my life; this would be right at the

top of that list,' said Letterman when he heard the song.

While they did not tour for *Songs of Surrender*, one was already in the works. Just as they did for *The Joshua Tree* in 2017, U2 had the idea of revisiting *Achtung Baby* on a tour for the album's 30th anniversary in 2021. However, with the pandemic still ongoing, they decided to wait, instead shifting their attention a couple of years later towards the anniversary of Zoo TV. With how the culture had shifted due to global politics over the last few years, U2 realized the themes of that original tour were still relevant. On modernizing that concept, Adam told *Esquire*, 'How do you update the Zoo TV concept? Because all the predictions of Zoo TV have come to pass: fake news, media overload, the MTV generation, wars fought on television with camera systems that could follow a missile down the street, as it was in the Iraq–Kuwait war at that time.'

During February 2018, the Sphere was announced as a new venue project collaboration between the Madison Square Garden Company and the Las Vegas Sands Corporation, which boasted a unique and innovative immersive experience. Construction began in September 2018 and was later temporarily halted in March 2020 due to the Covid-19 pandemic, finally opening three years later in September 2023. The Sphere was a technical marvel due to both its exterior and interior visual technology. A 366-foot-high and 516-foot-wide LED screen inside the venue wraps around the walls and ceiling, projecting 16K resolution imagery and 4D visual effects, with the outside featuring nearly 600,000 square feet of LED components that cover the building's entire exterior with full motion video.

Rumours that U2 agreed to perform a concert residency at the Sphere surfaced as early as July 2022, but the shows were not confirmed until February 2023 when U2 announced the residency in a commercial that aired during Super Bowl LVII. In the commercial, a spherical object hovers above several cities before landing in the desert, revealing a baby's face to all the people gathered there and confirming the residency as U2:UV Achtung Baby Live at Sphere. U2:UV would feature U2 playing *Achtung Baby* in its entirety, although not in sequence, as well as

several of their classic songs. In the lead-up to the Sphere residency, it was announced that Larry would not join his bandmates as he would need to recover from surgery, which would be the first time he had not played with the band since 1978. As U2 were committed to performing, Bram van den Berg from the Dutch band Krezip filled in for Larry. 'It's going to take all we've got to approach the Sphere without our bandmate in the drum seat,' said his bandmates, 'but Larry has joined us in welcoming Bram van den Berg who is a force in his own right.'

Many of the visual elements for U2:UV paid homage to Zoo TV. With the Sphere's interior screen projecting the inside of the Roman Pantheon before the concert, the show began with the band breaking through the walls while performing 'Zoo Station', a call-back to the opening of the earlier tour. The onscreen graphics of the Zoo TV version of 'The Fly' were supercharged in the Sphere, with the screen flashing words not just in front of the audience but above them as well. Effects also made the screen appear to change shape and dimension, making it seem like the ceiling was coming down.

However, U2:UV did more than just pay tribute, including breathtaking visuals not connected with Zoo TV that heightened the emotion and sensory experience of the songs. A kaleidoscopic art piece dedicated to Las Vegas icons during 'Even Better Than the Real Thing' created the sensation that the stage was lifting. Helicopters appeared on the screen to shine a spotlight on U2 during 'Vertigo', highlighting how the Sphere could blend live footage with produced video. During 'With Or Without You', the desert on the screen filled up with water as an orb floated towards the audience, surrounding them with a massive sepia-toned display of endangered species from Nevada that then burst into full dazzling colour during 'Beautiful Day'.

Even within a building designed to achieve maximum visual stimulation, U2 managed to find the intimate spaces within the concert. During a semi-acoustic segment in the middle of the show, the imagery on the screen was minimized with the attention then placed on the band members and the stage. Designed to resemble a record player, modelled after one designed by Brian Eno, the stage consisted

Bono, The Edge, Adam Clayton and Bram Van Den Berg perform at the Sphere, Las Vegas, 2023.

of LED panels that projected algorithmically generated 'colourscapes'. The centre of the stage also rotated to create the effect of a record player turntable turning. It took 18 months to develop U2:UV, resulting in an experience that expanded beyond Zoo TV to show audiences what Adam described as 'the relationship between the consumer economy and climate change' in which 'the art and artists have created a narrative that embodies communities. We're all part of the problem and the solution'. U2:UV ran for 40 shows from September 2023 through March 2024, earning critical acclaim both for U2's performances and for the Sphere's stunning technical prowess. Documenting their residency at the Sphere, U2 released the concert film *V-U2: An Immersive Concert Film* in September 2024. Directed by the Edge and his wife Morleigh Steinberg, the Edge said, 'The goal was to give the immersive moviegoers as close to the live U2:UV concert experience as possible – and then some.' 'We knew all the tremendous capabilities of the technology, but we didn't know what to expect from the process of making this film,' says Steinberg. 'The work became a true collaboration between band, artists, producers and technology teams. The end result is a cinematic experience that transports viewers into the energy and beauty of the live show.'

To celebrate the opening night of U2:UV on 29 September 2023, U2 released a new single called 'Atomic City'. Produced by Jacknife Lee and Steve Lillywhite, and recorded at Sound City Studios in Los Angeles, 'Atomic City' references Las Vegas' history of nuclear tourism during the 1950s. It also musically pays tribute to late 1970s post-punk and shares similarities with Blondie's 1980 Giorgio Moroder-produced hit 'Call Me', both of whom also get composer credit on 'Atomic City'. Though unable to play during U2:UV, Larry played drums on 'Atomic City' and appeared in the song's music video shot in Las Vegas. U2 performed the song from the Sphere during the Grammy Awards in February 2024, and released several remixes to promote it.

U2's emergence into a world beginning to be driven by social media had got off to a rocky start. However, by the time of their residency at the Sphere, they had proved that they were still a hugely popular and successful rock band, and their legacy remained intact.

This period of their career started off being rather challenging, but U2 would eventually bounce back bigger than ever, proving they could reinvent themselves to adapt to a new musical landscape. Though they had already achieved a legacy in which they could rest on their laurels, U2 still worked to explore new concepts and themes within their music. Even amid their fourth decade together, as sung in 'Atomic City', U2 remain committed to the ideal that has driven them since the beginning; if your dreams don't scare you, they're not big enough.

Bono, The Edge, Adam Clayton and Bram Van Den Berg perform at the Sphere with Lady Gaga, 2023.

Outro

After 50 years performing as a band, U2 show no signs of standing still

. Though they have had one foot firmly planted in their past, a position that has kept them grounded since being up-and-coming rockers playing around Dublin, they kept looking ahead with a vision that reached beyond. They introduced millions to the world they knew and grew up in, but U2 were also not afraid to push their limits as artists. With every new album came fresh ideas and a burning desire to discover more by doing things differently from before.

The drive and ambition that set U2 on their musical journey, like with every other young band, was born out of a necessity to break out into a world much larger than their own. Though countless bands have shared similar humble origins and aspirations, it takes much more to keep a band together during all that time.

What U2's legacy reveals about the music they created is that not only does it capture the spirit of the moment in which it was recorded, but the new sonic shapes these songs take on through U2's live performances and reimagined arrangements over the years reveal the reason these songs continue to live on: that they speak to our shared humanity. While many of U2's songs became hits and defining anthems of their time, with audiences coming together to make U2 a global rock phenomenon, those songs still continue to resonate decades later. Very few bands get the opportunity to release new music and perform live for as long and as consistently as U2 have. Luck and hard work is what gets a band signed, but only a few have that special something that keeps people listening for half a century.

The journey was not always easy. You cannot have a career as lasting, rich and storied as U2's and not stumble every once in a while. While a negative review or bad press can make some bands double down on a formula that had worked for them before, U2 were unafraid to explore new ideas. 'The thing is that there were better bands than us in Dublin back then – bands who looked better, played better, wrote better songs,' Bono told *Tidal* in 2014, 'but what we got from the Ramones and The Clash was that you could just pick up a mic and say something through your music … It's still the only reason U2 exists today.'

After 50 years, U2 still exists today and with their sights set towards the future as they wrap up recording a new album. Following a robust creative period celebrating their legacy and reflecting on how far they have come as a band, U2 is ready to prove (again) they can still surprise fans and audiences, both old and new. However, with age comes wisdom, and U2 are well aware where their music fits within the culture and that whatever they do next has to be on their terms. 'I don't think the world is waiting on the next U2 album,' Bono told *Mojo* in 2023. 'I think we have to give them a reason to be interested in it. I just want to write great tunes, because that's where U2 started – with big choruses, clear ideas. And let's go back there, but do it with some petrol and some matches.'

Whatever U2 do next will be anyone's guess, but the band is excited about the opportunity to reach audiences and listeners once again. Bono told *Mojo* that U2's next album would be a 'noisy, uncompromising' and 'unreasonable guitar record'. 'I announced it, without discussion,' said Bono, 'and Edge called me up and goes, "How unreasonable?" And I said, "As unreasonable as you're ready to take it."'

'I would love that to be the next U2 record!' the Edge told *Mojo*. 'The [Covid-19] lockdown was a very creative period for me, just in composing music. I don't want to jinx ourselves … but there's a lot of great material waiting. I think the guitar is coming back. I really feel it. And I would like to be part of that. I'd like to be in the vanguard of this resurgence of guitars.'

'We are turning the amps on,' said Adam. 'I certainly think the rock that we all grew up with as 16- and 17-year-olds, that rawness of those Patti Smith, Iggy Pop records … that kind of power is something we would love to connect back into.'

However, any new album, and a tour to support it, would need the entire band to get behind it. Approaching the end of his recovery from back surgery, Larry has been in the studio with the rest of his bandmates, working to put together the album.

No one could ever have imagined what U2 would accomplish since their first time playing together in 1976, and it has been a remarkable journey to watch unfold. Some fans have been with U2 since the beginning

as their story was being written, while others are new to the party. Regardless of when and how one comes to discover U2, the effect their music has had has been truly immeasurable.

However, at some point, U2 will end. When that will be and how far U2 still has to go on their journey, we can only wait and see. In the meantime, we still have a lot more great music to look forward to, and even when they do eventually stop, U2 have already left so much for us and future generations to enjoy. In that sense, will U2 ever really end? Depends on how you look at it.

But for myself, and for many others, U2 will be there until the end of the world.

Discography

Album: Boy
Released: 20 October 1980
Studio: Windmill Lane (Dublin)
Length: 42:52
Producer: Steve Lillywhite
Tracklist:

1.	'I Will Follow'	(3:40)
2.	'Twilight'	(4:22)
3.	'An Cat Dubh'	(4:46)
4.	'Into the Heart'	(3:27)
5.	'Out of Control'	(4:12)
6.	'Stories for Boys'	(3:04)
7.	'The Ocean'	(1:34)
8.	'A Day Without Me'	(3:12)
9.	'Another Time, Another Place'	(4:31)
10.	'The Electric Co.'	(4:47)
11.	'Shadows and Tall Trees'	(5:13)

Album: October
Released: 12 October 1981
Studio: Compass Point (Nassau);
Windmill Lane (Dublin)
Length: 41:05
Producer: Steve Lillywhite
Tracklist:

1.	'Gloria'	(4:14)
2.	'I Fall Down'	(3:39)
3.	'I Threw a Brick Through a Window'	(4:54)
4.	'Rejoice'	(3:37)
5.	'Fire'	(3:51)
6.	'Tomorrow'	(4:39)
7.	'October'	(2:21)
8.	'With a Shout (Jerusalem)'	(4:02)
9.	'Stranger in a Strange Land'	(3:56)
10.	'Scarlet'	(2:53)
11.	'Is That All?'	(2:59)

Album: War
Released: 28 February 1983
Studio: Windmill Lane (Dublin)
Length: 42:03
Producer: Steve Lillywhite
Tracklist:

1.	'Sunday Bloody Sunday'	(4:38)
2.	'Seconds'	(3:09)
3.	'New Year's Day'	(5:37)
4.	'Like a Song...'	(4:48)
5.	'Drowning Man'	(4:12)
6.	'The Refugee'	(3:40)
7.	'Two Hearts Beat as One'	(4:00)
8.	'Red Light'	(3:46)
9.	'Surrender'	(5:34)
10.	'40'	(2:36)

Album: Under A Blood Red Sky
Released: 21 November 1983
Studio: Red Rocks Amphitheatre (Morrison, CO); Freilichtbühne Loreley; (St. Goarshausen, Germany); Orpheum Theatre (Boston)
Length: 35:29
Producer: Jimmy Iovine
Tracklist:

1.	'Gloria'	(4:32)
2.	'11 O'Clock Tick Tock'	(4:34)
3.	'I Will Follow'	(3:36)
4.	'Party Girl'	(2:52)
5.	'Sunday Bloody Sunday'	(4:55)
6.	'The Electric Co.'	(5:18)
7.	'New Year's Day'	(4:29)
8.	'40'	(3:36)

Album: **The Unforgettable Fire**
Released: 1 October 1984
Studio: Slane Castle (County Meath);
Windmill Lane (Dublin)
Length: 42:38
Producer: Brian Eno; Daniel Lanois
Tracklist:

1.	'A Sort of Homecoming'	(5:28)
2.	'Pride (In the Name of Love)'	(3:48)
3.	'Wire'	(4:19)
4.	'The Unforgettable Fire'	(4:55)
5.	'Promenade'	(2:35)
6.	'4th of July'	(2:12)
7.	'Bad'	(6:09)
8.	'Indian Summer Sky'	(4:17)
9.	'Elvis Presley and America'	(6:23)
10.	'MLK'	(2:31)

Album: **The Joshua Tree**
Released: 9 March 1987
Studio: STS (Dublin); Danesmoate House
(Dublin); Melbeach (Dublin); Windmill Lane
(Dublin)
Length: 50:11
Producer: Brian Eno; Daniel Lanois
Tracklist:

1.	'Where the Streets Have No Name'	(5:38)
2.	'I Still Haven't Found What I'm Looking For'	(4:38)
3.	'With Or Without You'	(4:56)
4.	'Bullet the Blue Sky'	(4:32)
5.	'Running to Stand Still'	(4:18)
6.	'Red Hill Mining Town'	(4:52)
7.	'In God's Country'	(2:57)
8.	'Trip Through Your Wires'	(3:33)
9.	'One Tree Hill'	(5:23)
10.	'Exit'	(4:13)
11.	'Mothers of the Disappeared'	(5:12)

Album: **Rattle and Hum**
Released: 10 October 1988
Studio: Sun (Memphis); Point Depot
(Dublin); Danesmoate (Dublin); STS
(Dublin); A&M (Los Angeles); Ocean Way
(Hollywood)
Length: 72:27
Producer: Jimmy Iovine
Tracklist:

1.	'Helter Skelter'	(3:07)
2.	'Van Diemen's Land'	(3:06)
3.	'Desire'	(2:58)
4.	'Hawkmoon 269'	(6:22)
5.	'All Along the Watchtower'	(4:24)
6.	'I Still Haven't Found What I'm Looking For' (with The New Voices of Freedom)	(5:53)
7.	'Freedom for My People' (performed by Sterling Magee and Adam Gussow)	(0:38)
8.	'Silver and Gold'	(5:50)
9.	'Pride (In the Name of Love)'	(4:27)
10.	'Angel of Harlem'	(3:49)
11.	'Love Rescue Me' (with Bob Dylan)	(6:24)
12.	'When Love Comes to Town' (with B. B. King)	(4:14)
13.	'Heartland'	(5:02)
14.	'God Part II'	(3:15)
15.	'The Star-Spangled Banner' (performed by Jimi Hendrix)	(0:43)
16.	'Bullet the Blue Sky'	(5:37)
17.	'All I Want Is You'	(6:30)

Album: **Achtung Baby**
Released: 18 November 1991
Studio: Hansa (Berlin); Elsinore (Dalkey);
STS (Dublin); Windmill Lane (Dublin)
Length: 55:27
Producer: Daniel Lanois; Brian Eno
Tracklist:

1.	'Zoo Station'	(4:36)
2.	'Even Better Than the Real Thing'	
		(3:41)
3.	'One'	(4:36)
4.	'Until the End of the World'	(4:39)
5.	'Who's Gonna Ride Your Wild Horses'	
		(5:16)
6.	'So Cruel'	(5:49)
7.	'The Fly'	(4:29)
8.	'Mysterious Ways'	(4:04)
9.	'Tryin' to Throw Your Arms Around the World'	(3:53)
10.	'Ultraviolet (Light My Way)'	(5:31)
11.	'Acrobat'	(4:30)
12.	'Love Is Blindness'	(4:23)

Album: **Zooropa**
Released: 5 July 1993
Studio: The Factory (Dublin); Windmill Lane
(Dublin); Westland (Dublin)
Length: 51:15
Producer: Flood; Brian Eno; The Edge
Tracklist:

1.	'Zooropa'	(6:31)
2.	'Babyface'	(4:01)
3.	'Numb'	(4:20)
4.	'Lemon'	(6:58)
5.	'Stay (Faraway, So Close!)'	(4:58)
6.	'Daddy's Gonna Pay for Your Crashed Car'	(5:20)
7.	'Some Days Are Better Than Others'	
		(4:17)
8.	'The First Time'	(3:45)
9.	'Dirty Day'	(5:24)
10.	'The Wanderer' (with Johnny Cash)	
		(5:41)

Album: **Original Soundtracks 1**
(collaboration with Brian Eno under the name
Passengers)
Released: 6 November 1995
Studio: Westside Studios (London); Hanover
Quay (Dublin)
Length: 58:10
Producer: None credited
Tracklist:

1.	'United Colours'	(5:31)
2.	'Slug'	(4:41)
3.	'Your Blue Room'	(5:28)
4.	'Always Forever Now'	(6:24)
5.	'A Different Kind of Blue'	(2:02)
6.	'Beach Sequence'	(3:31)
7.	'Miss Sarajevo' (with Luciano Pavarotti)	(5:40)
8.	'Ito Okashi' (with Holi)	(3:25)
9.	'One Minute Warning'	(4:40)
10.	'Corpse (These Chains Are Way Too Long)'	(3:35)
11.	'Elvis Ate America' (with Howie B)	
		(3:00)
12.	'Plot 180'	(3:41)
13.	'Theme from The Swan'	(3:24)
14.	'Theme from Let's Go Native'	(3:08)

Album: **Pop**
Released: 3 March 1997
Studio: Hanover Quay (Dublin); Windmill
Lane (Dublin); The Works (Dublin); South
Beach (Miami)
Length: 60:09
Producer: Flood; Howie B; Steve Osborne
Tracklist:

1.	'Discothèque'	(5:19)
2.	'Do You Feel Loved'	(5:07)
3.	'Mofo'	(5:49)
4.	'If God Will Send His Angels'	(5:22)
5.	'Staring at the Sun'	(4:36)
6.	'Last Night on Earth'	(4:45)
7.	'Gone'	(4:26)
8.	'Miami'	(4:52)
9.	'The Playboy Mansion'	(4:40)
10.	'If You Wear That Velvet Dress'	(5:15)
11.	'Please'	(5:02)
12.	'Wake Up Dead Man'	(4:52)

Album: **All That You Can't Leave Behind**
Released: 30 October 2000
Studio: HQ (Dublin); Windmill Lane (Dublin); Westland (Dublin); Totally Wired (Dublin); South of France
Length: 49:25
Producer: Daniel Lanois; Brian Eno
Tracklist:
1. 'Beautiful Day' (4:06)
2. 'Stuck in a Moment You Can't Get Out Of' (4:32)
3. 'Elevation' (3:45)
4. 'Walk On' (4:55)
5. 'Kite' (4:23)
6. 'In a Little While' (3:39)
7. 'Wild Honey' (3:47)
8. 'Peace on Earth' (4:46)
9. 'When I Look at the World' (4:15)
10. 'New York' (5:28)
11. 'Grace' (5:31)

Album: **How to Dismantle an Atomic Bomb**
Released: 22 November 2004
Studio: Hanover Quay (Dublin); South of France
Length: 49:03
Producer: Steve Lillywhite
Tracklist:
1. 'Vertigo' (3:14)
2. 'Miracle Drug' (3:59)
3. 'Sometimes You Can't Make It on Your Own' (5:08)
4. 'Love and Peace or Else' (4:50)
5. 'City of Blinding Lights' (5:47)
6. 'All Because of You' (3:39)
7. 'A Man and a Woman' (4:30)
8. 'Crumbs from Your Table' (5:03)
9. 'One Step Closer' (3:51)
10. 'Original of the Species' (4:41)
11. 'Yahweh' (4:21)

Album: **No Line on the Horizon**
Released: 27 February 2009
Studio: Riad El Yacout (Fez); Hanover Quay (Dublin); Platinum Sound (New York); Olympic (London)
Length: 53:44
Producer: Brian Eno; Daniel Lanois; Steve Lillywhite
Tracklist:
1. 'No Line on the Horizon' (4:12)
2. 'Magnificent' (5:24)
3. 'Moment of Surrender' (7:24)
4. 'Unknown Caller' (:03)
5. 'I'll Go Crazy If I Don't Go Crazy Tonight' (4:14)
6. 'Get On Your Boots' (3:25)
7. 'Stand Up Comedy' (3:50)
8. 'Fez – Being Born' (5:17)
9. 'White as Snow' (4:41)
10. 'Breathe' (5:00)
11. 'Cedars of Lebanon' (4:13)

Album: **Songs of Innocence**
Released: 9 September 2014
Studio: Electric Lady (New York); Pull (New York); The Church (London); Assault & Battery (London); Shangri-La (Malibu); The Woodshed (Los Angeles); Strathmore House (Killiney)
Length: 48:11
Producer: Danger Mouse; Paul Epworth (add.); Ryan Tedder (add.); Declan Gaffney (add.); Flood (add.)
Tracklist:
1. 'The Miracle (of Joey Ramone)' (4:16)
2. 'Every Breaking Wave' (4:13)
3. 'California (There Is No End to Love)' (4:00)
4. 'Song for Someone' (3:47)
5. 'Iris (Hold Me Close)' (5:20)
6. 'Volcano' (3:15)
7. 'Raised by Wolves' (4:06)
8. 'Cedarwood Road' (4:26)
9. 'Sleep Like a Baby Tonight' (5:02)
10. 'This Is Where You Can Reach Me Now' (5:06)
11. 'The Troubles' (with Lykke Li) (4:46)

Album: **Songs of Experience**
Released: 1 December 2017
Studio: Electric Lady (New York); The
Garage (Topanga, California); Shangri-La
(Los Angeles); Strathmore House (Killiney);
Neptune Valley (Los Angeles); Hanover
Quay (Dublin); Windmill Lane (Dublin);
The Woodshed (Los Angeles); Uno Mas
(Brentwood, Tennessee); Waterloo (Los
Angeles); The Church (London)
Length: 51:07
Producer: Jacknife Lee; Ryan Tedder; Steve
Lillywhite (add.); Andy Barlow (add.); Jolyon
Thomas (add.); Brent Kutzle (add.); Paul
Epworth (add.); Danger Mouse (add.); Declan
Gaffney (add.)
Tracklist:

1.   'Love Is All We Have Left'   (2:41)
2.   'Lights of Home' (with HAIM)   (4:16)
3.   'You're the Best Thing About Me'
                                       (3:45)
4.   'Get Out of Your Own Way'   (3:58)
5.   'American Soul'   (4:21)
6.   'Summer of Love' (with Lady Gaga)
                                       (3:24)
7.   'Red Flag Day'   (3:19)
8.   'The Showman (Little More Better)'
                                       (3:23)
9.   'The Little Things That Give
        You Away'   (4:55)
10. 'Landlady'   (4:01)
11. 'The Blackout'   (4:45)
12. 'Love Is Bigger Than Anything
        in Its Way'   (4:00)
13. '13 (There Is a Light)'   (4:19)

Album: **Songs of Surrender**
Released: 17 March 2023
Studio: Shangri-La (Los Angeles); The Village
(Los Angeles); Metropolis (London); Harbour
Island
Length: 165:50
Producer: The Edge
Tracklist:

1.   'One'   (3:36)
2.   'Where the Streets Have No Name'
                                       (4:17)
3.   'Stories for Boys'   (2:51)
4.   '11 O'Clock Tick Tock'   (3:58)
5.   'Out of Control'   (4:09)
6.   'Beautiful Day'   (3:53)
7.   'Bad'   (5:31)
8.   'Every Breaking Wave'   (5:11)
9.   'Walk On (Ukraine)'   (4:07)
10. 'Pride (In the Name of Love)'   (3:57)
11. 'Who's Gonna Ride Your Wild Horses'
                                       (5:17)
12. 'Get Out of Your Own Way'   (3:27)
13. 'Stuck in a Moment You Can't
        Get Out Of'   (4:34)
14. 'Red Hill Mining Town'   (5:02)
15. 'Ordinary Love'   (3:13)
16. 'Sometimes You Can't Make It
        on Your Own'   (5:00)
17. 'Invisible'   (4:23)
18. 'Dirty Day'   (3:57)
19. 'The Miracle (of Joey Ramone)'   (3:29)
20. 'City of Blinding Lights'   (4:55)
21. 'Vertigo'   (3:29)
22. 'I Still Haven't Found What I'm
        Looking For'   (4:15)
23. 'Electrical Storm'   (4:13)
24. 'The Fly'   (4:02)
25. 'If God Will Send His Angels'   (5:14)
26. 'Desire'   (2:56)
27. 'Until the End of the World'   (4:44)
28. 'Song for Someone'   (3:48)
29. 'All I Want Is You'   (4:28)
30. 'Peace on Earth'   (4:22)
31. 'With Or Without You'   (3:14)
32. 'Stay (Faraway, So Close!)'   (5:03)
33. 'Sunday Bloody Sunday'   (4:13)
34. 'Lights of Home'   (4:20)
35. 'Cedarwood Road'   (3:24)
36. 'I Will Follow'   (3:40)
37. 'Two Hearts Beat as One'   (4:08)
38. 'Miracle Drug'   (3:35)
39. 'The Little Things That Give
        You Away'   (4:52)
40. '40'   (3:03)

Picture Credits

Every effort has been made to trace and acknowledge the copyright holders. We apologize in advance for any unintentional omissions and would be pleased, if any such case should arise, to add appropriate acknowledgment in any future edition of the book.

Getty Images: 2,37, 48, 96, 98 both (Rob Verhorst/Redferns); 4, 30, 44, 53, 72, 74 (Pete Still/Redferns); 6, 19, 22 both, 23, 25 (Virginia Turbett); 8 (David Cooper/Toronto Star via Getty); 10 (Vincenzo Lombardo/Redferns); 12 (Steve Rapport); 14; 17, 41 both (Lisa Haun/Michael Ochs Archives); 20 (Randy Bachman); 24 (L.Cohen/WireImage); 26 all, 27 (Peter Noble); 28, 42, 64 (Paul Natkin); 32, 34 (Koh Hasebe/Shinko Music); 38, 120 (Ebet Roberts/Redferns); 47 (Clayton Call/Redferns); 50 (Erica Echenberg/Redferns); 55, 91 (Aaron Rapoport/Corbis); 57 (Peter Carrette Archive); 58 (Dino Ignani); 61, 66, 80 (Independent News and Media); 62 (Staff/Daily Mirror/Mirrorpix); 68 (Dave Hogan/Hulton Archive); 71 (Bob King/Redferns); 77 (Ralph Dominguez/MediaPunch via Getty); 78 Neil H Kitson/Redferns); 81 (George Rose); 82 (Bettmann); 85, 86 bottom (Gie Knaeps); 86 top, 110 (Frederic GARCIA/Gammo-Rapho via Getty); 89 ARNAL/Gamma-Rapho via Getty); 95 (David M Bennett); 99, 109 (Andrew Fox/Corbis via Getty); 100,126 (Mick Hutson/Redferns); 102 (Dave Benett); 105 (Pictures Ltd./Corbis via Getty); 106 top (Larry Busacca), 112, 141 (Paul Bergen); 116, 118, 156, 163, 234 (Brian Rasic); 122, 138, 159 top (Dave Hogan); 124 bottom (SGranitz/WireImage); 129 (Tim Mosenfelder/CORBIS via Getty); 131 (Brenda Chace/Stringer); 133, 197 (KMazur/WireImage); 134 (Georges Gobet/AFP via Getty); 136 (Kevin Westenberg/Live 8 via Getty); 137 (Frank Micelotta/ImageDirect); 142 (Jeff Kravitz/FilmMagic, Inc); 144 (Lester Cohen); 148 (TEPHEN JAFFE/AFP via Getty); 150; 153; 154 (Tim Mosenfelder); 159 bottom (Chris Graythen); 164, 169 (Andy Willsher/Redferns); 171 (Epsilon); 173; 174 (Vera Anderson/WireImage); 176 (Kevin Winter);178 (Justin Sullivan); 180 (Debra L Rothenberg); 186 (Keystone/Hulton Archive); 190 (Jeff J Mitchell); 195 (Simone Joyner); 191 (Paul Morigi); 202 (Michael Buckner/Variety/Penske Media via Getty); 222 (Lex van Rossen/MAI/Redferns); 240 (San Francisco Chronicle/Hearst Newspapers)

Alamy: 93 (David Hickes); 106 bottom; 114, 211 (Barry King); 208 Andreas Rentz/Getty Images; 124 top (F.Rabelo-Jornal do Brasil/Associated Press); 147 (Pictorial Press Ltd); 160 Richard Beland); 166 (Rainer Jensen/DPA Picture Alliance Archive); 183 (Archivo ABC/Inés Baucells); 184 (Pacific Press Media Production Corp.); 188 (Kevin Estrada/MediaPunch); 189 (Rich Fury/Invision/AP); 192 (Associated Press); 200, 201, 208 (Everett Collection Inc); 204 (UPI); 207 (AP Photo/Nathan Howard); 213, 214, 216 (Anne-Marie Forker); 219 (Leon Farrell/Rolling-News.ie); 220 (PA Images); 224 (PARAMOUNT PICTURES); 232 (Moviestore Collection Ltd); 238 (AAP Image/Sam Wundke)

Acknowledgements

Thank you so much to U2 for all the great music and memories over the years. Twenty-five years ago, when I bought my first U2 CD at 13, *All That You Can't Leave Behind*, I would never have guessed where my journey with the band would take me. Writing this book was a wonderful opportunity, and I am grateful for the people in my life who have been with me during it. Thank you to Robert Nichols for taking a chance on me, leading with expert guidance all the way, and I trust that I brought you the best U2 book you could have hoped for because of that. Thank you to Lisa Dyer and Claire Browne for shepherding this book into its final form, which looks stunning and is something of which I am so immensely proud. Thank you to the Little Museum of Dublin for your wonderful U2 exhibit that was inspirational to me as I began writing the book and for gifting me your book of Patrick Brocklebank's photos. Thank you to my friends who have supported me over the years; Steven Anderson, Lily Bacon, Adam Balling, Paul Birza, Keith Bjorklund, Paul Blanding, Andy Bugay, Rene Calvo, Shawn Campbell, Cécile Carrié, Craig Cobane, Aaron Cohen, Mimi Cole, Mary Conway, Bethany Doerfler, Tim Donovan, Craig Duff, Juliann Esqueda, Josh Friedberg, Al Gabor, Joe Held, Taylor Hodgkins, Karen Johnson, Melissa Karalis, Carolyn Kassnoff, Debra, LaRocco, Jennifer Lizak, Jean Mahony, Dan Menna, Scott McKenna, Kyle Sanders, Eric Sinclair, Amelia Vargas, and Anne Zender. My biggest thanks and gratitude, as always, goes to my family.

References

Features and Interviews

'1976-09-25', *U2Songs.com*.

'All U2 songs by number of times played in concert', *U2gigs.com*.

'Bono has "combative relationship" with late dad', *Yahoo! Life*, 28 October 2022.

'Bono planning to reinvent U2 sound', RTÉ, 2 January 2007.

'Bono Tells Story of U2's "Bullet the Blue Sky"', *Rock & Roll Hall of Fame*, 18 May 2016.

'Bono's War on Poverty & AIDS', CBS News, 7 April 2005.

'The Enduring Chill: Bono and the Two Americas', *Propaganda*, 1 December 1986.

'Exclusive: Bono Reveals Secrets of U2's Surprise Album "Songs of Innocence"', *Rolling Stone*, 9 September 2014.

'The Hype Changes Their Name to U2', *U2.com*.

'Inductees: U2', *Rock & Roll Hall of Fame*.

'The Origins of U2's "One Tree Hill"', *The Sound*, 8 March 2019.

'September Event 2014', Apple, 9 September 2014.

'Showing all tours for U2', *U2gigs.com*.

'U2 – the early years: "There was a presence, a magnetism…"', *Uncut*, 12 September 2014.

'U2's Bono and the Edge perform in Ukraine subway station', *The Guardian*, 8 May 2022.

Barbour, David, 'U2:UV: Music of the Sphere', *Lighting & Sound International*, November 2023.

Bell, Jonathan, 'How to conquer the Atomic City: the story behind U2 at the new Las Vegas Sphere', *Wallpaper*, 27 September 2023.

Benitez-Eves, Tina, 'Watch: U2 Sift Past, and Present, Lyrics on "Sort of Homecoming" Documentary', *American Songwriter*, 17 March 2023.

Bernstein, David, 'Broadway's "Spider-Man": The Full Story', *Chicago Magazine*, 8 November 2010.

Blashill, Pat; DeCurtis, Anthony; Edmonds, Ben; et al., 'All That You Can't Leave Behind: U2', *Rolling Stone*, 11 December 2003.

Bono, 'World debt angers me', *The Guardian*, 16 February 1999.

Burgoyne, Patrick, 'U2 Linear: It's Not a Music Video', *Creative Review*, 14 April 2009.

Cameron, Keith, '"Bono Was Absolutely Right …" U2's Edge Interviewed!', *Mojo*, 28 March 2023.

Catchpole, Chris, 'U2 New Album Exclusive: "I just want to write great tunes, because that's where U2 started, with big choruses, clear ideas"', *Mojo*, 17 November 2023.

Chilton, Louis, 'Bono shares new ballad written in tribute to Italy's coronavirus victims', *The Independent*, 18 March 2020.

Chowdhry, Amit, 'Apple Launches Tool to Remove Free U2 Album', *Forbes*, 22 September 2014.

Dalton, Stephen, 'How the West Was Won', *Uncut*, October 2003.

de Whalley, Chas, 'Another Time: The Inside Story of U2's Very First Record', *Record Collector*, 1 September 2004.

DeCurtis, Anthony, 'U2's Edge and Adam Clayton Look Back on Two Decades of Hit Albums with Few – If Any – Regrets', *Revolver*, December 2000.

DeRiso, Nick, '20 Years Ago: U2 Pay Tribute To 9/11's Fallen at the Super Bowl', *Ultimate Classic Rock*, 3 February 2022.

Doyle, Tom, '"It will be called Songs for Fighting!" U2 Interviewed', *Mojo*, 14 March 2023.

Dye, David, 'Bono on World Café', National Public Radio, 14 October 2014.

Eccleston, Danny, 'Back in God's Country', *Mojo*, August 2017.

Eccleston, Danny, 'Too Tough to Die', *Mojo*, January 2015.

Edwards, Gavin, 'U2's "Bad" Break: 12 Minutes at Live Aid That Made the Band's Career', *Rolling Stone*, 10 July 2014.

Espen, Hal, 'U2 Interview: Oscar Hopes, That Unfinished Album, Anxiety About Staying Relevant', *The Hollywood Reporter*, 12 February 2014.

Falsani, Cathleen, 'Herstory', *U2.com*, 29 June 2017.

Fielder, Hugh, 'New "Zooropa" Revue', *Pulse!*, October 1993.

Finn, Kevin, 'Stephen Averill: Collaboration, identity and design – backstage with U2', *TheSumOf*, 20 November 2023.

Fletcher, Tony, 'U2: The Pride of Lions', *Jamming!*, 1 October 1983.

Frenette, Brad, '"Futuristic spirituals": Daniel Lanois talks about recording the new U2 album', *National Post*, 10 March 2009.

Fricke, David, 'U2 Shoot for Year's End', *Rolling Stone*, 8 April 2002.

Gallo, Phil, 'U2 and sharp keys: Soul star, Bono

tops with "O Bro"', *Variety*, 27 February 2002.

Gardner, Elysa, 'Download U2 song, fight global disease', *Chicago Sun-Times*, 1 February 2014.

Glynn, Paul, 'Berlin Wall: "Germany was first reunited on the dancefloor"', *BBC*, 8 November 2019.

Goldstein, Steve, 'Music Writer Recalls U2's History With Arizona's Political Scene', *KJZZ 91.5 Phoenix*, 19 September 2017.

Golsen, Tyler, 'How Brian Eno first started working with U2', *Far Out*, 13 May 2022.

Graff, Gary, 'Adam Clayton Breaks Down U2's "Songs of Surrender"', Teases Upcoming Documentary Projects'. *Billboard*, 7 March 2023.

Greene, Andy, 'U2's the Edge on "All That You Can't Leave Behind" at 20: "It Was a Natural Moment to Reboot', *Rolling Stone*, 23 October 2020.

Grow, Kory, 'Edge: U2 Have "50 Ideas" for Next Album', *Rolling Stone*, 29 March 2016.

Guerin, Harry, 'U2 tell Dublin: "The boys are back in town"', *RTÉ*, 6 November 2018.

Halperin, Shirley, 'Island's Chris Blackwell on Signing U2 in 1980: Their "Music Was a Little Rinky-Dink"', *The Hollywood Reporter*, 20 December 2010.

Hammershaug, Bjørn, 'Age of Innocence: U2's Dublin Beginnings', *Tidal*, 23 October 2014.

Heath, Chris, 'U2: "It's About Self Respect"', *Rolling Stone*, 17 August 2000.

Helms, Colin, 'Interview with The Edge', *CMJ*, 30 October 1998.

Hiatt, Brian, 'Taking Care of Business', *Irish Independent*, 4 April 2009.

Horowitz, Steven J, 'U2 to Debut Edge-Directed Immersive Concert Film "V-U2" at Sphere Las Vegas', *Variety*, 21 August 2024.

Ives, Brian, 'Ryan Tedder on U2's Next Album: "I've Never Seen Them This Focused"', *Radio.com*, 20 May 2016.

Klein, Joshua, 'Brian Eno and Daniel Lanois Remember the Making of U2's Unforgettable Fire', *Pitchfork*, 23 October 2009.

Kot, Greg, 'U2 at Soldier Field: Still searching for answers at "Joshua Tree"', *Chicago Tribune*, 5 June 2017.

Kreps, Daniel, 'See U2, Springsteen, Kacey Musgraves "Stand Up for Ukraine" on Livestream', *Rolling Stone*, 9 April 2022.

Mayer, Catherine, 'U2's Mission to Save Music', *Time*, 18 September 2014.

McGovern, Kyle, 'Grammy Hall of Fame 2014 Inductees: U2, Neil Young, Run-D.M.C., Rolling Stones, and More', *Spin*, 3 December 2013.

McGrath, Shaughn, 'U2 Achtung Baby – a look

back', *AMP Visual*, 15 November 2011.

McGreevy, Ronan, 'Ex-U2 manager says iTunes album release a mistake', *The Irish Times*, 6 June 2015.

McLean, Craig, 'Achtung Vegas: The Inside Story of U2 at the Sphere', *Esquire*, 13 October 2023.

Meyers, Carly, 'Interview with the Edge', *CFNY-FM*, 6 September 2017.

Moody, Nekesa Mumbi, 'Slew of music stars to perform at Super Bowl', *The Desert Sun*, 31 January 2002.

Mueller, Andrew, 'U2 – The Joshua Tree Remastered (R1987)', *Uncut*, 10 December 2007.

O'Donnell, Kevin, 'Bono reveals details of U2's new album "Songs of Experience"', *Entertainment Weekly*, 12 October 2015.

O'Hagan, Sean, 'The Wanderers', *The Guardian*, 14 February 2009.

O'Hare, Colm, 'Easter Rising', *Hot Press*, 4 September 2001.

Parker, Lyndsey, 'Dave Letterman on the sweet song Bono and the Edge wrote for him: "Makes the first 35 years of being in television well worth the effort"', *Yahoo! Entertainment*, 16 March 2023.

Paul, Larisha, 'Bono Recalls His Mother's Unexpected Death – and How the Loss Turned Him to Music: "We Rarely Thought of Her Again"' *Rolling Stone*, 20 September 2022.

Phillips, Lior, 'From Beyoncé to U2: Songwriter and Producer Ryan Tedder Chases Euphoria in the Studio', *Consequence of Sound*, 17 October 2016.

Power, Ed, 'PopMart: Were U2 making a joke or was the joke on them?',*The Irish Times*, 30 October 2018.

Quinn, Ben, 'French police still haven't found what U2's looking for', *Irish Independent*, 15 July 2004.

Rapp, Allison, '25 Years Ago: U2 Concludes Elaborate PopMart Tour', *Ultimate Classic Rock*, 21 March 2023.

Rees, Paul, 'The Q Interview: Rick Rubin', *Q*, October 2009.

Reynolds, Steve, '30 years ago, U2's Bono visited Ethiopia "on the quiet"', *World Vision*, 22 October 2015.

Sandberg, Marian, 'Willie Williams on U2's Innocence + Experience, Part 1', *Live Design*, 3 June 2015.

Saraceno, Christina, 'Bono Meets Bush', *Rolling Stone*, 15 March 2002.

Sisario, Ben, 'For U2 and Apple, a Shrewd Marketing Partnership', *The New York Times*, 9 September 2014.

Smirke, Richard, 'U2 Producer Andy Barlow

'On "Songs of Experience": The Album Changed Massively After Trump Got Elected', *Billboard*, 6 December 2017.

Stancavage, Sharon, 'In the Name of Simplicity', *Entertainment Design*, August 2001.

Sweeney, Éamon, 'Chris Blackwell: "I was very impressed with U2 – Paul McGuinness dressed in a suit"', *The Irish Times*, 9 June 2022.

Thrills, Adrian, 'Cactus World View', *NME*, 14 March 1987.

Tingen, Paul, 'Robbie Adams: Recording U2's Achtung Baby & Zooropa', *Sound on Sound*, March 1994.

Treisman, Rachel, 'U2's Bono and the Edge held a concert in a Kyiv subway station in support of Ukraine', National Public Radio, 10 May 2022.

Tyrangiel, Josh, 'Mysterious Ways', *Time*, 22 November 2004.

Weiss, Joanna, 'Flag football', *The Boston Globe*, 2 February 2002.

Willman, Chris, '"Kennedy Center Honors" TV Review: U2, George Clooney and Amy Grant Master Their Reaction Shots as Other Stars Do the Saluting', *Variety*, 28 December 2022.

Willman, Chris, 'Larry Mullen Jr Says U2 Tour Is Not Likely for 2023, as He Faces Surgery', *Variety*, 28 November 2022.

Winfrey, Oprah, 'Oprah Talks to Bono', *O, The Oprah Magazine*, April 2004.

Zaleski, Annie, 'The Day U2 Had Their First Band Rehearsal', *Ultimate Classic Rock*, 26 September 2021.

Books

Alan, Carter, *Outside Is America: U2 in the US* (Boston: Faber and Faber, 1992).

Bono and Michka Assayas, *Bono: In Conversation with Michka Assayas* (New York: Riverhead Books, 2005).

Bono, *Surrender: 40 Songs, One Story* (New York: Alfred A. Knopf, 2022).

Boyd, Brian and Stokes, Niall *U2: Songs + Experience* (London: Carlton Books Ltd, 2018).

Brocklebank, Patrick, *U2: 1978–1981, Photographs by Patrick Brocklebank* (Dublin: The Little Museum of Dublin, 2022).

Calhoun, Scott, ed., *Exploring U2: Is This Rock 'n' Roll?: Essays on the Music, Work, and Influence of U2* (Lanham, Maryland: Scarecrow Press, 2012).

Flanagan, Bill, *U2 at the End of the World* (New York: Delacorte Press, 1995).

Graham, Bill, *U2: The Early Days* (New York: Delta, 1990).

Macdonald, Bruno, ed., *The Greatest Albums You'll Never Hear: Unreleased Records by the World's Greatest Musicians* (London: Aurum, 2014).

McGee, Matt, *U2: A Diary* (London: Omnibus Press, 2011).

Morgan, Bradley, *U2's The Joshua Tree: Planting Roots in Mythic America* (Guilford, Connecticut: Backbeat, 2021).

Parkyn, Geoff, *U2 Touch the Flame: An Illustrated Documentary* (New York: Perigee Books, 1987).

Stokes, Niall, *North Side Story: U2 in Dublin 1978–1983* (Dublin: Hot Press, 2013).

Stokes, Niall, *U2: Into the Heart* (New York: Thunder's Mouth Press, 2001).

U2 with Neil McCormick, *U2 by U2* (New York: HarperCollins, 2006).

U2, *The Complete Lyrics, Vol. 1* (1979–1988) (U2 Limited, 2023).

U2, *The Complete Lyrics, Vol. 2* (1991–2024) (U2 Limited, 2024).

Media

Bono & the Edge: A Sort of Homecoming with Dave Letterman (Streaming, directed by Morgan Neville, Disney+, 2023).

Classic Albums: U2 – The Joshua Tree (DVD, directed by Philip King and Nuala O'Connor, Isis Productions, 1999).

From the Sky Down (DVD, directed by Davis Guggenheim, Universal Music Group, 2011).

Innocence + Experience: Live in Paris (DVD, directed by Hamish Hamilton, Universal Music Group, 2016).

Kiss the Future (Streaming, directed by Nenad Cicin-Sain, Paramount Pictures, 2023).

PopMart: Live from Mexico City – 'The Road to Sarajevo' (DVD documentary featurette, produced by Ned O'Hanlon. Universal Music Group, 2007).

Rattle and Hum (DVD, directed by Phil Joanou. Paramount Pictures, 1988).

U2, Liner notes, *All That You Can't Leave Behind* (20th anniversary CD box set. Universal Music Group, 2020).

U2, Liner notes, *The Joshua Tree* (20th anniversary CD/DVD box set. Universal Music Group, 2007).

U2 Live at Red Rocks: Under a Blood Red Sky (DVD, directed by Gavin Taylor. Island Records, 1984).

U2-Y: A Design Story (Podcast series, hosted by Gareth and Steve Averill. 2023).

About the Author

Bradley Morgan, a media arts professional based in Chicago, is the author of *U2's The Joshua Tree: Planting Roots in Mythic America* and *Frank Zappa's America*. He manages partnerships for CHIRP Radio 107.1 FM and is the director of the station's music film festival. He also interviews authors of music and pop-culture books for the *New Books Network* podcast. He enjoys travelling to places with music history.